BABIES IN
THE LIBRARY!

Jane Marino

The Scarecrow Press, Inc.
Lanham, Maryland, and Oxford
2003

SCARECROW PRESS, INC.

Published in the United States of America
by Scarecrow Press, Inc.
A wholly owned subsidiary of The Rowman & Littlefield Publishing Group, Inc.
4501 Forbes Blvd., Suite 200, Lanham, Maryland 20706
www.scarecrowpress.com

PO Box 317
Oxford
OX2 9RU, UK

British Library Cataloguing in Publication Information Available

Library of Congress Cataloging-in-Publication Data

Marino, Jane.
  Babies in the library! / Jane Marino.
    p. cm.
  Includes bibliographical references and index.
    ISBN 0-8108-4576-8 (alk. paper)
    1. Children's libraries—Activity programs—United States. 2.
Libraries and infants—United States. 3. Libraries and toddlers—United
States. 4. Libraries and caregivers—United States. I. Title.
Z718.2.U6 M37 2003
027.62'5—dc21

1000   2002012022

To all the babies whose smiles,
songs, and hugs have brightened my life.

CONTENTS

❶

BABIES IN THE LIBRARY

In the last decade, children's librarians, realizing the value of reaching out to very young children, have begun library programs which are focused on this very valuable patron group, specifically children aged two and under. Similarly, there have been books written about programs for babies and toddlers, statewide and national organizations and initiatives have sprung up to support the idea of early childhood literacy and to support various library programs that have literacy and the love of language for baby as their goals. The goals of these programs are to promote literacy and the love of language from the start of a baby's life, to spotlight for parents and caregivers the value and necessity of singing, speaking, and reading to babies and to model for parents the best ways to do that. The purpose of this book is to throw an even bigger spotlight on the youngest of babies who need the benefits of library programs and to encourage librarians to welcome them into their libraries.

It is important to pay attention to babies who are under two years old, especially in library programs, but there is just as big a need to pay specific attention to the babies who are less than a year old. These babies, who are called prewalkers here, have for years been considered too young for the library and in too many libraries, they still are considered too young. But those who are working with babies in libraries and elsewhere know that the repetition of rich language presented in a warm, loving environment is some of the best, most nutritious food a baby can receive. As more evidence is uncovered about how much babies can learn from the minute they are born, it is imperative for us as librarians and child advocates to pay particular attention to them.

We can do that in three important ways: by making the library a welcoming place for parents of babies; by offering and presenting effective library programs that the babies and their parents will enjoy, and by modeling for parents and other caregivers of babies the best way to share the rhymes, songs, and books best suited for their babies. The rhymes included in these programs are both traditional and original. Many of them have appeared in other collections. Here, however, they are presented both for librarians and other programmers with an eye to their developmental value. Therefore, they are presented in two groups of programs. The first group has programs using rhymes for prewalkers, babies from birth to around a year old who are not yet walking confidently on their own. The second group has programs using rhymes for young walkers, babies up to the age of around two, who can participate in and enjoy rhymes, games, and songs that involve the whole body, encourage imitation, and engage the imagination.

For each developmental level a list of the rhymes under specific labels precede each group of programs. Those rhymes, how they are defined and used, will be further discussed in the introductions for each of the two sections, prewalkers and walkers. Although it is true that all babies would enjoy all these rhymes, they are divided here into these developmental levels to make it easier for programmers to choose and use them. The ways that babies react to rhymes and songs in a group is vastly different from the way they enjoy a rhyme or song when it is shared one on one from a grownup who loves them.

There are many ways parents can bring these rhymes home and incorporate them into their day. In the familiar environment of the home, the rhymes become an accompaniment to baby's day. There are changing table/bathtub rhymes, food/meal rhymes, car/outdoor rhymes, nighttime rhymes. There will be a small section containing rhymes not used in any of the programs, including some additional puppet rhymes and rhymes that are best for a special occasion or holiday. These divisions are intended to make it easier for parents to choose and for you to recommend to parents, although there are never any hard and fast rules where babies are concerned. Parents have reported to me that a fussy baby in a car seat loved it when her mom sang our program's opening song, *Hello Song* to her while they were driving in the car!

Resources for both programmer and parent are included. There are bibliographies of programming books, picture books, collections of rhymes and songs, lists of audio and video items as well as a list called "Baby's Bookshelf," which contains some of the best bets for baby. There will also be a list of some of the national initiatives and programs that encourage emergent literacy. These programs embrace the idea that sharing songs and rhymes and books with babies and enabling their parents to do that most effectively is the best way to raise children to become readers who love books.

WHY A BABY PROGRAM?

This is a question that many busy, overburdened children's librarians still ask. Their library's programming roster may already be filled with preschool story hours, outreach to nursery and grade schools, craft and film programs, book discussion groups, and teen programs. Many libraries have no programs at all for children under eighteen months old. Others who have baby programs set a minimum age of six months or twelve months. When we, as children's librarians, set an arbitrary minimum age limit, we are saying to parents that if their baby is four or five months old, he's not "old" enough for the library. Along with the sad fact that we've excluded a baby who would have benefited from the rhymes and songs we have to share with him, we are saying to parents that reading to babies or sharing rhymes with babies should wait until they are old enough.

Busy as we all are, it's wrong for us as librarians to rationalize the exclusion of babies from programs until they reach a certain magical age. Research has shown that babies learn and absorb from the moment they are born and even before that. They undergo a startling period of growth and development in the first year of their lives and during that time they are absorbing everything around them. Why should we, as librarians, wait? Mothers and fathers talk to their babies from the minute they lay eyes on them. And babies respond. We can enrich that communication. We can help parents entertain their babies with ways that need nothing more than a quiet moment, a warm lap, and a baby eager to hear the voice he loves. We can also help parents soothe that baby when he is fussy and crying, and nothing they do seems to help. Parents, especially young parents, may reach a level of frustration with a crying baby much more quickly when they feel unable or badly equipped to soothe him. If we in our libraries let that first year of baby's life go by without inviting young parents in or reaching out to them, we are missing a golden and unique opportunity. Mem Fox, in her book, *Reading Magic*, states that "Children's brains are only 25 percent developed at birth. From that moment, whenever a baby is fed, cuddled, played with, talked to, sung to or read to, the other 75 percent of its brain begins to develop. . . . The foundations for learning to read are set down from the moment a child first hears the sounds of people talking, the tunes of songs and the rhythms and repetitions of rhymes and stories" (Fox 13, 14).

The library is one of the few places in our world where everyone walks through the door on an equal footing. We can gather parents and babies together here in a way quite different from any other place in town. In the library, parents and caregivers are there simply to enjoy their babies, share language with them, and learn from them. They will have the chance to meet other parents and caregivers and their babies will meet other babies. Dorothy Butler, author of *Babies Need Books*, stated in a speech before the New York Public Library/New York University Early Childhood Conference in 1989, that "Babies and small children need precision, beauty, lilt and rhythm, and the opportunity to look and to listen, both at will and at length, as well as to touch feel and smell. Words are finely tuned instruments which must be encountered early" (Butler, 156).

Here is our opportunity to create that first, early encounter with the precision and beauty of the words in Mother Goose rhymes, songs, and picture books for baby. Many of the books and articles that are published on early childhood literacy speak of "pre-reading" experiences as being a valuable component of nurturing that literacy. A library program for infants and toddlers is just such a "pre-reading" experience. While its goal is not to teach anything, it introduces rhymes and songs and books to baby and parent in an atmosphere that is nonjudgmental and nonthreatening so that baby and parent can enjoy the rhymes and songs and make them part of their lives. Think of it as your first opportunity to equip parents who may be young, frustrated, and lacking in ways to communicate with their babies. In an article for *Five Owls Magazine* in May/June 1999, Julie Schumacher and Hilary Stecklein point to language as the important stimulus for brain development. But, they further point out, it's not just any language. "Language learning is best accomplished within a context of nurturing care. It is the attention, the reciprocal delight, and the dance of interaction between child and adoring adult that turns spontaneous noise into meaningful communication" (Schumacher, 5).

Although that statement makes a strong case, many librarians resist programming to babies because it is a program with small, sometimes invisible, results. But what makes it so vital is that it is the beginning of the road to reading that will be filled, not with giant leaps, but with baby steps. For the babies and parents on that road, the baby steps they are taking are vitally important. Cori Trudeau, the managing editor of *The Five Owls*, writes in the March/April 2001 issue of *The Five Owls for Parents* about the baby program she and her son Ray attend at their local library. "[The librarian] sing-speaks loudly and clearly with lots of arm gestures and facial expressions. Ray falls in love with her every time we go and can't keep his eyes off of her. . . . This is a learning experience for me, as well as Ray" (Trudeau, 1). A young mother once told me that my program taught her how to talk to her baby. She really didn't know how to communicate with her baby, she told me, and the baby program she attended gave her rhymes and songs that made it easier for her and that, she felt, helped her to be a better parent. For me and other librarians who program to babies, moments like these are giant leaps on the path of baby steps because it demonstrates the power of rhyme, the power of song, the power of words.

HOW TO BRING BABIES INTO YOUR LIBRARY

The first step to bringing babies into your library is to make the library a comfortable and welcoming place for them and their parents. Start by taking stock of the children's room and see if there are books, magazines, and music to entice babies and their caregivers. Books for babies should include board books, such as the books by Rosemary Wells about that consummate toddler, Max; nursery rhyme collections, such as the beautiful collection by Clare Beaton, *Mother Goose Remembers* (Barefoot Books, 2000), and picture books, such as the classic bedtime title, *Goodnight Moon*, by Margaret Wise Brown (Harper & Row, 1947). There are lists for each of these categories in the appendix.

There are also some really good magazines for parents as well as one or two for baby. Here are some of the best.

American Baby is published by Primedia Magazines, Inc., 249 West 17th St., New York, NY 10011. With its focus on both babies and pregnant mothers, it has recommendations on things to buy for babies, advice on child rearing, recipes for pregnant mothers as well as other features.

Babybug, published by Carus Publishing Company, Cricket Magazine Group, 315 Fifth St., Peru, IL 61354, is a unique publication aimed specifically at baby. With its small size and slightly stiff pages, as well as simple stories and rhymes and simple illustrations, it's a perfect vehicle for lap sharing between parent and child.

Child, also a parenting magazine, is published by Gruner & Jahr Printing and Publishing Co., P.O. Box 3176, Harlan, IA 51593-0367. Its areas of information include child development, discipline, lifestyle, health & fitness, food & nutrition, media, and a section called "Just for You."

Ladybug the Magazine for Young Children, also published by Carus, is aimed at slightly older tots, children from age two to six. Filled with child-friendly poems, stories, and songs, it beckons to the parent to read aloud to a toddler and to the beginning reader, with its slightly oversized print in some stories, rebus stories, and short, rhymed poetry. There's even some music and some stories told in comic or storyboard format.

Parenting, published by The Parenting Group, Inc., 350 Fifth Ave., New York, NY 10036, is aimed at parents of babies as well as expectant parents. It has tips for baby feeding and crying, child development issues, dinner recipes as well as fashions for the expectant parent and editors' picks on toys.

Parent and Preschooler Newsletter, a small unassuming publication by the North Shore Child & Family Guidance Center, 480 Old Westbury Road, Roslyn Heights, NY 11577-2215, is just eight pages long. Containing only two articles, they are nonetheless extremely informative and useful to both parents and professionals. There are also craft and recipe suggestions, and the last page, entitled "Library Resources" has short book reviews centered on a theme so they are not necessarily new books, but they are still useful and good choices.

Music is another essential component of your parent and baby-friendly children's room. Babies are born music lovers, and they will love everything. John Feierabend and Luann Saunders have produced three wonderful CDs—one for each of the first three years of a baby's life. *Round and Round the Garden, Music in my First Year* is the first in this series and contains simple songs and rhymes and bounces that are perfect for both parent and programmer. These recordings join the ranks of such children's specialists as Hap Palmer, Ella Jenkins, and Bob McGrath. From classical to the more "traditional" children's music, there are lots of good selections. Most of the titles listed in the appendix are available in both cassette and CD.

Most important of all is the atmosphere you create within your children's room that will signal to parents and caregivers of babies that they are welcome there. Is it easy for them to get strollers and carriers in and out the door? Are there chairs for both parents and tots? Is your board book collection easily accessible to young hands? Is your picture book area somewhat separated from the rest of your children's area so parents and caregivers of babies and toddlers will feel comfortable enough to let their children play and interact without fear of being a disruption? Do you have lists of recommended books for both babies and parents? Do you have lists of books on issues important to parents, such as a new baby in the house or starting school? Do you have information on other programs for babies and toddlers in your town as well as information on nursery schools or head start programs? Do you have baby-proof toys and a safe area in which to play with them that has no sharp edges, exposed outlets, or small items that can go into baby's mouth?

The atmosphere you created will go a long way to say to parents and their babies, "You're welcome here. This is your library."

CREATING A BABY PROGRAM

Before beginning a baby program in your library, take a serious look at the programs your library already offers and try to find the best spot for the new program to fit. If your programming schedule is already extraordinarily overcrowded, you may have to let something go or consolidate what you already offer. Two programs may duplicate offerings to the same age group. You may have a program that is not being well attended or that has outlived its usefulness to the community. Make sure you also consider the needs of this new audience. Although babies may be the smallest of your patrons, they can be the busiest. They have meal times and nap times that are always changing. Their parents may have other siblings that have to be considered. So they are not as flexible as their older counterparts may be. The middle of the morning seems to be the best for most babies and toddlers. Whether you schedule the program on a weekday or weekend morning, babies and parents will enjoy the songs, rhymes, and books in your program much more at this time of day.

As you prepare for your baby program, learn as much as you can about the baby programs that others have done. If there are other libraries in your system or county that already offer an infant program, visit them and watch their programs. Although each librarian should find a style that suits her best, the ideas you can get from watching other programs will be invaluable. There are also a few recordings and videos that offer ideas and tips about sharing rhymes and songs with baby, and they are listed in the appendix.

Once you have decided on a day and time for your program, reach out to the other early childhood agencies in your community, the nursery schools and daycare centers, to make them aware of it. They are among the best resources for you to reach parents of babies and toddlers. Spread the word in your library as well, mentioning it to every young mother or father who comes into the children's room. These methods are just as valuable as adding your program to the calendar or library's monthly newsletter, where it may be overlooked by young parents who may be unaware of this new program's existence.

Find a room or spot in your library most conducive to a program of this kind. Babies need a smaller space than preschoolers or primary graders for many reasons. They are, of course, smaller, so a smaller space than you would use for preschool story time will create a sense of intimacy that will make both babies and caregivers feel comfortable. As babies grow and become walkers (and runners) providing as little space as possible for them to run, climb, and otherwise become distracted will work to your advantage. Try to find a space that is quiet and away from the traffic of other library patrons. Clear away, as completely as possible, all toys, puzzles, and books that will prove a distraction during the program. Clear away chairs, also. So even if all you have is a corner of the children's room, hide the toys, move the chairs, and have as clear a spot as possible. Have a few stools ready for grandparents and other older caregivers, but encourage everyone else to sit on the floor with you. Have the grownups form a circle with you, with their babies sitting on their laps or, if they are walkers, sitting directly in front of them.

The circle you're creating with the babies and their grownups does several things. It enables everyone in the program to see everyone else. It puts everyone on an equal footing and eliminates the idea of you as the programmer and them as the anonymous audience. This is a sharing program, where everyone sings and chants and enjoys the books together. It puts you as the programmer as close as possible to your audience and with babies, that's an important point. They need to be able to see you and their caregivers. In this setup, they can. Once everyone is comfortably settled, you're ready to begin.

The first few months of any new program are the most difficult as you find a comfortable spot for it in your schedule and you make connections with the people in your community who will benefit most from it. So don't be discouraged as the program suffers growing pains. This program may, and probably will, take longer to establish itself than other programs since it is so different from anything you may have had before. If attendance is small or parents and other caregivers seem uncertain about their role in the program, don't give up. Talk to them both before and after the program to make sure they know how welcome they are and how much you value their attendance.

PREWALKERS AND WALKERS

The sample programs that are offered in this book are offered for two distinct developmental groups: prewalkers and walkers. These terms were created as a way to easily identify which program is best for baby, according to his developmental level, rather than his age. Prewalkers are babies who are not yet walking confidently on their own. So a prewalker can be anywhere in age from newborn to twelve or thirteen months of age or even a few months older. Although this seems like a wide age range, the rhymes that are used for this group focus on the fact that the babies are more comfortable sitting on their grownups' laps, rather than being ready to get up and go, the way a walking baby would be.

Walkers are babies who *are* walking confidently on their own. They no longer have to think about the mechanics of walking. They are sure of the sturdiness of their two little legs to hold them up and carry them around.

The developmental focus of these two groups is effective for a number of reasons. First, you as a programmer know what you have in your group. You can prepare for the program confident that all the rhymes, songs, and books you use will be appropriate for the babies in that program. When you mix these two groups together, you run the risk of the older babies becoming bored with the soft, gentle prewalker rhymes or the younger babies mixed into a walker group becoming overwhelmed by the activity rhymes that are physically beyond them. When you base the division on age rather than physical development, the dividing line, wherever you make it, will end up with a group of toddlers with a mixed bag of abilities.

If a caregiver and baby are placed in the group that is the most appropriate for them, they will feel comfortable, and from one program to the next, know what kinds of things to expect. Parents and caregivers who feel comfortable and happy about a program for their babies will be most likely to return.

Parents and caregivers of prewalkers have different concerns and issues than the parents and caregivers of walkers. First of all, this may be their first visit to the library in a long time. If this baby is their first child, they will be both nervous and proud about introducing her to you and other babies and parents. They are there not only to enjoy the program but to learn the rhymes and songs they may never have heard or may have forgotten. They won't know how their baby will react to the program or even if it's worth it to them to be a part of it. Make sure to spend a little extra time greeting these newcomers, introducing yourself, and making sure they know where the program will take place and when it will start.

Parents and caregivers of walking babies have a wider world to consider. Now that their babies, who will have an average age of about eighteen months, have started moving confidently around, they won't sit still for the quieter, calmer prewalker rhymes that worked so well just six months ago. These little movers and shakers need to be up and about, jumping from one rhyme and song to the next with the speed and variety of a typical *Sesame Street* program.

Since there is a strong physical link between the rhymes and the baby, by replacing age range in your groups with developmental levels, you are reinforcing that physical link. If a baby is not yet walking, she will respond much more positively to a bouncing lap rhyme where nothing more is demanded of her than to sit on her caregiver's lap and enjoy the rhythm. But if that baby finds herself, because she is now twelve months old, in an older, more active group of babies who can walk when she cannot, she *and* her caregiver will feel out of place and uncomfortable.

Many parents will perceive the developmental labels as some kind of test and insist that a baby can walk when that baby has only begun to stand or pull himself up. When they attend the walker program, however, they clearly see the physical differences between their baby and the others in the group. So it's important to make it clear to parents that walkers must really walk and it's okay if their baby is an age the parent may consider "too old" but is still a prewalker.

Although there are people, both parents and programmers, who believe in combining the two groups, I don't think this will lead to a successful outcome for your program. Although this group believes that babies learn from older children who, in turn, "model" for the younger babies, I think the benefit of this modeling is far outweighed by the dominance that these older children will display, effectively taking over the program from the babies. By paying separate attention to prewalkers, the modeling role is filled by the parents or caregivers without the older tot, who by his sheer energy or exuberance, becomes the primary source of focus.

REGISTRATION

As I have talked to many librarians about doing baby programs, the issue of registration seems to be one of their biggest concerns. Registration for this program is vital to its success. Although you may feel pressure from your community or from administrators to welcome everybody who wants to attend, the risks of having too large a group far outweigh the benefits of allowing everybody into the program. First and foremost, this is an interactive and sharing program. You should not be, nor should you think of yourself as, an entertainer. Your role as programmer is to introduce rhymes, songs, and books to babies and caregivers so they can share them both in the program and again at home. With a big group, the interactive aspect of the program is removed simply because you need to keep control, make sure everyone can hear and see and worry about having enough room for everybody.

When you institute registration for your program, you accomplish many important things. First, you will know how many people are coming. As simple as that sounds, it is important to the program's success. If you have only five babies signed up for your prewalker class, for example, and they are all under six months old, you may plan a vastly different program than you would for ten or fifteen babies ranging in age from four months to thirteen months. Second, you will be able to go around the group and allow everyone to introduce themselves and their babies, another element in the program vital to its success. By encouraging and allowing everyone to identify and introduce himself, you are making them partners in your program. They can no longer be an anonymous member of an audience. Now, you know their names and their babies' names. They are active participants. In a smaller group, you can have an opportunity to introduce each rhyme and song and your audience will hear you and pay attention to you. You can (and should) use the babies' names throughout the program, reinforcing the intimacy you've established with the small group and your introductions.

How to conduct registration is another matter. Consider your other programs and whether or not you have registration for them. Whether you have a phone-in system or require your parents to register in person or use a lottery system is not really important. What is important is to be consistent and allow as many people as possible to participate in the program, so that somebody who may not have been able to come to one program can come to another program.

THE RHYMES AND SONGS

As you look at the sample programs for the prewalkers, you will see a variety of rhymes that are indexed according to what they do and how they should be used. Why divide and label them? They are divided and labeled because they are being used in a group setting, a situation vastly different than that of Mom or Dad alone with baby. Babies in a group respond best to a group of rhymes that are varied in pace and rhythm. You as a programmer want a group of happy babies and comfortable grownups and that group will become easily bored, for example, if you did nothing but sing one lullaby after another. But an even, balanced mixture of different kinds of rhymes will keep the entire group happy. Prewalkers will be anywhere from newborn to around a year, so clapping songs, bouncing songs, and lap-riding songs will all be enjoyed at different levels, even within this program.

For walkers, the rhymes are divided and labeled to reflect the wider world a walking baby lives in, where things around him are coming more sharply into focus and they can be included in the rhymes you choose. They have begun to notice and identify the people around them, animals, food, and the world outside. By using all of these things in your rhymes, you are incorporating things that are familiar to a walker, which makes it easier for parent and baby to use them again at home.

Encourage your parents and caregivers to use many of the rhymes and songs they've heard at your program at home. You can even make a handout with some of the rhymes on them for parents to take home.

PREPARING YOUR PROGRAM

Five prewalker and five walker programs are included in this book. They each contain approximately sixteen rhymes or songs and two suggested books. They are complete and intended for your use just as they are presented. They have a variety of the kinds of rhymes discussed above in them and there are brief explanations and introductions for each. You can also substitute one of the rhymes suggested for another and/or add any of your own. The main goal you should have, as you prepare your program, is to create it so that you feel comfortable and confident doing it. Practice the rhymes and songs so you will be comfortable and confident. I have indicated recordings where you can listen to most, if not all of the songs I have suggested. Listen to them, sing along with them, and if you are really nervous about singing alone—although babies and their parents are the easiest, most noncritical audiences around—use the recordings in the program. Practice the rhymes as well. Copy them onto index cards and bring the cards into the program with you. Index cards give you the flexibility to change the order of the rhymes and songs that you're doing and eliminate the worry and distraction of having to hold sheets of paper or relying on your memory.

Don't use a rhyme you haven't practiced. Even for the most seasoned programmer, using a rhyme you've never said out loud, at least once, is a recipe for disaster. So run through the program several times; carry the cards around with you; listen to the recordings. Become as comfortable as possible with the material. When you've practiced, you can remove the worry of knowing the material and concentrate on enjoying the babies. But that doesn't mean you have to remove the cards. Use them in every program.

There are also two books suggested for each program. Practice the books, as well. Be prepared for a vastly different reaction from your baby audience than you get from preschoolers and older children. Babies listen in a very different manner than older children do. In a pre-walker group, although you will have urged your parents and caregivers to gather their babies back into their laps for the book, that doesn't always mean the babies look or even listen to what you are reading. Many of them will, but there will be some who won't. Don't worry or think the experience is not a success. Babies are listening even when they don't seem to be listening. More importantly, though, when you ask the parents and caregivers to gather up their babies and help them focus attention on the book, you will have their attention as well. As you read the book aloud, you model for the grownups how to read a picture book, and they will enjoy it as much as the babies. Having enjoyed the book, they will be eager to read it to their babies as well. That is the primary reason for giving them that chance immediately following your reading. When you hand a picture book to each grownup, you're saying, "Go ahead, it's your turn. Enjoy this time with your baby." And they will. Each baby in this kind of parallel lap-sharing time will also react differently to the book being read to them, which is an eye-opener to all the grownups in the group. When they see, first, how well their babies listen in a group and then how well they've done reading to their own baby, they will leave with increased confidence in their ability to do this at home.

There is a more detailed description of the programs at the beginning of each chapter on both prewalker and walker programs. But certain rules of thumb hold true for both groups. First of all, be flexible. Don't feel you must use a particular song or rhyme when you can clearly see it isn't going well. Although two books are suggested for each program, if the group is really restless use one. Second, make everyone in the group feel comfortable. You can do this in several ways. Make sure you've welcomed everyone and given them an opportunity to introduce themselves and their babies. Make clear from the beginning how the program will proceed. Tell parents when they register what day and time the program will take place, so they will show up on time. Make sure to answer any questions they may have. If they don't ask, elicit questions, especially when the program is new.

Registration is a good time to describe the program, both its elements and its length. Issues like siblings, showing up late or leaving early, food, or toys may come up at registration. Siblings, whenever possible, should be welcomed into the program, especially when the parent cannot attend without them. As a programmer, acknowledge and welcome the siblings and make them feel like the "big" kids they are. Invite them to do the rhymes and sing with you, so they won't feel as if they're stuck in a "baby" program, giving them an excuse and temptation to act out. Baby's food and toys, on the other hand, should not be welcomed. Bottles and treasured blankets should be the exception to this rule. But favorite stuffed dolls or other toys, as well as Cheerios and sippy cups, can quickly become sources of contention and distraction.

As the program begins, quickly but firmly announce whatever ground rules you may have. First, announce this as a language enrichment program in which you will share rhymes and songs with them and their babies. Please assure the parents and caregivers that their babies may not want to stay for the whole program and that it's okay for parents to take them out if they start crying or fussing. Explain to the adults that all rhymes will be done twice and encourage them to join in with you as you sing and say the rhymes and gently remind parents that the time to chat is after the program, not during it.

Second, make yourself comfortable. Dress as if you're going to be sitting on the floor with babies, with flat shoes and comfortable pants. Have everything you need—cards, books, and puppet—in a bag that's easy to carry and use.

Third, maintain your sense of humor. Remember that not everything will go as smoothly as you may wish, but most things will certainly go better than you would imagine. Look past the failures and celebrate the small successes.

These three elements—flexibility, comfort, and humor—are the three most important tools you can bring to this program. They will lead to a successful program as much as good rhymes, songs, and books.

TO THEME OR NOT TO THEME

Many, if not most librarians, who program to children of all ages feel very strongly about the issue of theme-based programming. The idea of building a program around the multitude of themes, from apples to zoos, that float around on the ocean of library programs is so attractive that many librarians would never think of programming without one. Other librarians feel they must have a theme or they haven't produced a proper program. Themes have their place. They are a useful framework around which to build a program. They give you an opportunity to use a song to reinforce a book or to string together two or three books or several rhymes in order to celebrate spring, explore numbers and letters, or have a Valentine's party during story time. In the walker programs that are presented here, the three or four pretend rhymes that are contained in each program are about the same thing, whether it's food or the outside.

But themes, especially overriding themes, do not have a place in infant programming, especially with prewalkers. The program's main goal is language enrichment. As a programmer, you should use the best rhymes and songs available, not the ones that match a theme. The rhymes and songs contained in the sample programs in this book were chosen for their quality.

Babies don't care about themes. Prewalkers certainly do not have any frame of reference in which to appreciate any theme you may use, and their parents want rhymes that are easy to remember and repeat, not necessarily ones that celebrate Groundhog Day. Although the pretend rhymes, as previously mentioned, may follow the same idea, they are not rhymes I wouldn't have used anyway. They all follow the same tests of quality I use for any rhyme. They have wonderful language, a bouncing rhyme, and they are fairly easy to remember and take home. They would also work all by themselves; they are not dependent on the theme they support. And if I choose to throw in a different rhyme that had nothing to do with anything, I am pretty confident that nobody in the program would really care, especially the two year olds.

Librarians who love and use themes are certainly welcome to pick and choose the books, rhymes, and songs in this book to create one, but it would be more for their enjoyment than the babies'.

FLANNEL BOARDS, PUPPETS, AND REALIA

Although flannel boards are fun to use, babies under the age of two are not ready to be the kind of formal audience they need to be in order for a flannel board story to succeed. Many babies simply don't understand that you're putting those pieces up on the board to tell a story. Many of them want to pull them off the board or touch them. That kind of distraction can be a big detriment to the success of your story. When you use a picture book with walkers, many of them want to come right up and stand in front of you, sit in your lap, or even help you turn the pages. But with a book, you have a little more flexibility to deal with these distractions. Welcome the lap-sitters, but raise the book a little bit higher so that the rest of the group can see over the standing baby, and gently hold the page down so it won't be turned prematurely.

Puppets can work if you use them wisely. Whatever puppet you use should have the ability to appear and disappear at will. So hide them in a bag until they make their appearance and return them to the bag once they've had their moment in the spotlight. Don't use too many. One or two puppets can add a nice touch. A puppet for every rhyme or song and your interactive, sharing program becomes a show. Use puppets only with walkers. There are puppet rhymes included in all the walker programs as well as some names of puppet manufacturers included in the appendix.

ABOVE ALL, TRY IT!

Many librarians have great trepidation about babies in the library. Sadly, many have preconceived notions that may not match with reality. Don't let that happen to you! Despite your fears or misgivings about doing a program like this, give it a try. This book gives you all the tools you need. As long as you have a good group of rhymes, songs, and books and a willingness to try, you're off to a good start. The first time a baby smiles at you or "falls in love" with you, you'll be hooked for life. Good luck. Try the programs, and you're on your way.

REFERENCES

Butler, Dorothy. "Saying it Louder" *School Library Journal*, September 1989. Vol. 35. no. 13, 155–159.

Fox, Mem. *Reading Magic: Why Reading Aloud to our Children Will Change their Lives Forever* (San Diego: Harcourt 2001) 13–14.

Schumacher, Julie, Julie & Hilary Pert Stecklein, M.D. "Nurturing Language Development in Children" *The Five Owls for Parents*. May/June 1999.

Trudeau, Cori. "Boogie Books" *The Five Owls for Parents*. March/April 2001. Vol 3, no. 4, p.1.

PREWALKER PROGRAMS

WHAT WORKS FOR PREWALKERS

The programs contained in this section use rhymes especially suited for prewalkers. They are divided into four categories: lap rhymes, clapping rhymes, self rhymes, and lullabies. The rhymes are divided and labeled in order to make it easier for the programmer to switch around rhymes found in the programs and to create other programs outside of the five ready-to-go programs contained here. The lap rhymes, both traditional Mother Goose rhymes as well as original rhymes and songs, constitute the bulk of a prewalker program. They range in activity level from simply inviting the adult caregiver to hold baby on their lap and bounce the baby to the rhythm of the rhyme, with perhaps some clapping or pointing to parts of the baby, to lifting the entire baby into the air several times during the song. Clapping and self rhymes are short and simple, focusing on the baby, with more clapping, patting, and rubbing of baby. Although only a few of these rhymes are used during each prewalker program, they are the easiest for caregivers and parents to learn and they should be introduced as rhymes that are easy to take home and use during the course of a baby's day. Lullabies are the final category and are always perfect for baby, whether prewalker or walker. At least two are introduced in each program and their classic, soothing words and music have a remarkably calming effect.

The true success for the program lies in the order in which the rhymes are presented, so as you become comfortable with prewalkers and want to make your own variations on the programs presented here, try to follow the same basic format and order of the rhymes. All the rhymes used in the programs are listed right before the programs to make it easier for you to choose them.

What makes these rhymes work so well for prewalker babies? They are filled with rhythm, whether spoken or sung. They engage at least some physical activity. The little stories they tell do not go beyond the scope of what baby knows. They generally focus on baby himself. There's lots of bouncing, hand-clapping, and lap-riding. A lullaby will soothe baby; a clapping, bouncing rhyme will engage baby. And it will elicit a big grin or giggle when baby is lifted high in the air and back to the parent's arms.

THE FRAMEWORK OF THE PROGRAM

The philosophy of a prewalker program is to engage both baby and parent or caregiver. Although its primary purpose may be to introduce rhymes and songs to baby, the parent or caregiver is the secret ingredient in making these rhymes and songs a regular part of baby's life. As you welcome them, encourage the adults who attend your programs to sing and say the words with you. Make sure the adults know how important they are to the success of the program, not just in the library, but at home, too.

In the programs presented here, you'll see that the rhymes are introduced, not just as something to do at that moment, but as something to bring home, too. The value of the parents' participation is one reason why each rhyme is done twice. It not only reinforces the words and rhythm or melody in the parents' minds, but it gives them an opportunity to join you the second time around. Second, it gives them a sense of ownership of the program. They know what to expect, at least to a certain extent, and they can depend on that. Babies recognize the rhymes and songs as soon as they hear them. Many babies who have attended my prewalker programs burst into huge smiles as soon as we start singing our *Hello Song*. They know where they are. The *Good-Bye Song* uses the same melody and format as the *Hello Song*, so it also quickly becomes a favorite. Babies care about themselves and they are comfortable with what they know. With these favorites, you will always be repeating something they know. For parents, it also gives them a sense of recognition and comfort. They can return to the program knowing the hello and good-bye song and a few others. The more rhymes they know, the more likely they'll be eager to join in.

Generally, the programs for prewalkers as they are presented here will last from twenty to twenty-five minutes. To engage a group of babies and their caregivers for that long requires a nice mix of different kinds of rhymes both spoken and sung topped off by a book and a couple of lullabies. All of the songs included here can be found on many of the recorded collections listed the Appendix. Although many of these rhymes can and should be sung, they'll also be successful if you chant them instead. Whenever possible, the songs within these programs are accompanied by the name of a recording where it can be found. If singing along with a tape or CD works better for you, these recordings can be your partner in song. In several instances, the recording noted has the tune with the traditional words to the song, not the words of the song in the program. But listening to the recording will still put the melody into your head before the program begins.

BEGINNING THE PROGRAM

As you begin each program, welcome and thank the parents, grandparents, babysitters, and caregivers who have taken the time to attend your program. Make sure to tell them what an important thing they are doing with their babies and that this time together will be both fun and rewarding for the two of them. Introduce yourself and give everyone in the group an opportunity to introduce him- or herself and baby too. Make sure grandparents or other visitors and siblings get introduced as well. Describe your program as a language enrichment program in which you will all be singing and saying rhymes and songs together, listening to books, and reading together. Remind them that you need their participation in order to make the program a success and that is why you'll be doing each rhyme twice: once for them to hear it and once for them to join in. After a few programs, they'll soon know many of the rhymes you do. Continue to do them twice anyway. Not only is it fun to repeat a favorite, it's wise to follow a pattern that you have established. After each rhyme, lead the group in enthusiastic applause. Babies this young may not know how to clap, but they love the applause. Many will think the group is clapping for them alone, a wonderful, self-affirming thought. Soon, they'll be giving themselves a hand, too. As you introduce each rhyme, say a few words of introduction or explanation. There are suggestions for these included in the programs themselves. Limit the remarks to how the grownups should hold their babies, or how the rhyme you're introducing can be used at home. If you go on too long, you'll lose the group's attention.

ENDING THE PROGRAM

Toward the end of the program is the time to read a book or two to the group. Two books are suggested for each of the prewalker programs. These are specifically recommended for the prewalker group. They are short enough to hold baby's attention, gentle enough for parent and child to share at home, and many of them also come in board book form. Although you will find that not every baby will pay attention to your reading of the book, keep reading anyway. There will always be some who will listen and there may even be a few who will recognize what you're reading. There may be a baby like the little boy in one prewalker group, who immediately lay down on his tummy upon hearing the words of *Goodnight Moon*, since that was his naptime book.

In each program, you'll see a suggestion to hand out board books to parents to share with the babies immediately after the "formal" reading of the book. This will accomplish a number of things. It will give parents and caregivers a chance to practice what they have just seen you do: reading out loud to their babies. It also gives you an opportunity to highlight the board books your library owns, so parents see them as something they can bring home and use with their baby. All too often, parents think of their prewalker babies as "too young" to be read to. Giving your parents an opportunity right in the program to read to their babies will reinforce just the opposite notion. It also gives everyone a break from the formal flow of the program, a valuable thing with a bunch of babies and young parents.

Many parents and caregivers see this time as an opportunity to chat once they are finished with the book, as their baby crawls off to socialize with the baby next to them. Other adults keep on reading and eagerly take another book once the first is done. Have the board books ready to hand out to each adult–child pair and leave a few extra on the floor for babies who want to "read" another book. If you want to expand your board book collection, a list of favorite board books is included.

Once this informal read-to-me section is completed, invite the parents to close the books they've been reading, and gather their wandering babies back onto their laps so the group can sing a lullaby. Two are suggested for each program, but if the group's tolerance is waning, just do one. You can be the best judge of what the group you have that particular day can tolerate. After the lullaby, make any announcements, such as the date of the next program or the next registration date. End the program with a good-bye song. Invite your grownups to stay and read with their babies and, of course, to take home as many board books as they'd like.

This will be a program to which parents and caregivers will be happy to return week after week. They will feel truly special knowing this program has been designed just for them. They will appreciate this unique invitation to become a lifelong library user.

PREWALKER RHYMES LIST

Lap-Riding/Action Songs
Alley-Oh
Away up High
Baa Baa Black Sheep
Baby Dear, Come Out to Play
Baby, Go Round the Sun
Flying Man
From Wibbleton to Wobbleton
Here We Go Up, Up, Up
Hey Diddle Diddle
Jack and Jill
Jack Be Nimble
Leg Over Leg
Let's Take a Walk
Little Frog

London Bridge
Mother & Father & Uncle John
Muffin Man
Noble Duke of York
One, Two, Three, Four, Five
Rickety, Rickety Rocking Horse
Ride a Cock Horse
Riding on My Pony
Riding the Merry-go-Round
Rigadoon
Rooster Crows
Say, Say, Oh Baby
This Is the Way the Farmer Rides
To Market
Tommy O'Flynn

Trot, Trot to Boston
Way Up High in the Apple Tree
What'll We Do with the Baby-O

Clapping Rhymes
Baby a Go-Go
Clap Hands, Clap Hands
Clap Your Hands
Great A, Little a
Handy Spandy
Hickety Pickety
One, Two, Buckle My Shoe
Pat-a-Cake
Pease Porridge Hot
Roly Poly

Self Rhymes
Catch a Wee Mouse
Diddle Diddle Dumpling
Exercises, Exercises
Good-Bye Song
Hello Song
Milkman, Milkman

Pitty Patty Polt
Round About
Round and Round the Butter Dish
Round and Round the Garden
Round and Round the Haystack
Rub a Dub Dub
Rub a Dub Dub, Who's in the Tub?
Shoe the Old Horse
These are Baby's Fingers
This Little Pig

Lullabies
Bye Low, My Baby
Dance to Your Daddy
Go to Sleepy Baby-Bye
How Many Miles to Babylon?
Hush-a-Bye
Lavender's Blue
Rock-a-Bye Baby
See Saw Margery Daw
Star Light Star Bright
Twinkle Twinkle

PROGRAM #1

The two rhymes that are used to begin and end this program will be the same in each of the prewalker programs. The first is a greeting rhyme and that's a good idea in any program, but especially here, when parents of new babies are perhaps starting a library program for the very first time. This rhyme sets the tone for the program and shows them, along with the introductions described earlier, how important a formal beginning can be. The familiarity of the hello and good-bye rhymes will bring comfort to babies and parents and help them claim ownership of this program. The recording indicated here will give you the melody that is shown under the title, but with its traditional words, but there is also a separate track available which will play the melody alone.

Hello Song
(melody: London Bridge)

Hi, hello and how are you?
How are you?   *Help baby to wave*
How are you?   *throughout the song.*
Hi, hello and how are you?
How are you today?
(*Toddler Tunes*)

The exercises chant is simply a fun, easy way to get things going and the first of many quick, easy rhymes that parents and caregivers will bring home and use with baby. The first time you introduce this rhyme acknowledge that some babies won't like to have their arms lifted up and down to this chant. So, start gently with this rhyme, saying it softly and slowly.

Exercises, Exercises

Exercises, exercises   *Lift baby's arms gently*
Let's all do our exercises.   *in the air to the rhythm*
Exercises, exercises   *of this rhyme.*
Let's all do our exercises.

The next rhyme that is used here is sung to a familiar tune and can be heard on Priscilla Hegner's recording, *Baby Games*. Her rendition of it is a good model and this will be a wonderful way to follow the first two rhymes. With its welcoming first line and lots of clapping and bouncing, it really gets both parents and babies involved. This rhyme is probably the longest you'll ever use in a prewalker program. You should still do it twice.

Say, Say, Oh Baby

Say, say, oh baby,
Come here and clap with me   *Hold baby on lap*
And bring your happy smile   *and do what the song*
Bounce on my lap so free.   *tells you to do.*
Shake, shake your hands, now.
Shake, shake your bottom too.
And shake your tootsies ten.
Let's do it again.
(*Baby Games*)

The bulk of the program incorporates first a couple of clapping rhymes and then some lap-riding/action songs. Clapping rhymes pick up the pace of the program just a bit, encouraging parents to join in with a simple action. These rhymes are traditional ones, both with a great rhythm that is reinforced by clapping hands. Acknowledge that most prewalkers cannot clap by themselves, but they love to watch their parents clap. Remember to do these short rhymes twice.

Hickety Pickety

Hickety pickety, my black hen.   *Parents help babies clap hands.*
She lays eggs for gentlemen.
Gentlemen come every day
To see what my black hen doth lay.

Great A, Little a

Great A, Little a   *Parents help babies clap hands*
Bouncing B,   *or bounce baby on lap.*
The cat's in the cupboard
But she can't see me.

The first two lap-riding/action songs involve no more action than baby riding on adult's knees or laps. They are traditional rhymes and even if parents and caregivers don't immediately know them, they are easy to learn, so parents will learn them quickly and should enjoy them.

For this first rhyme, encourage parents to put their babies up on their knees. Baby can face their caregiver or away from the caregiver toward the middle of the circle.

To Market To Market

To market, to market,   *"Ride" baby on knees or lap.*
To buy a fat pig.
Home again, home again,
Jiggity, jig.

To market, to market,
To buy a fat hog.
Home again, home again,
Jiggity, jog.

For this next rhyme, tell parents to keep their babies right where they are, up on their knees or in their laps. For smaller babies, they should face parents so they can be cradled. Bigger babies can sit up and face toward the group.

Rickety, Rickety Rocking Horse

Rickety, rickety rocking horse,	*"Ride" baby on knees.*
Over the hills we go.	
Rickety, rickety rocking horse,	*Gently rock baby back in lap*
Giddy-up, giddy-up, whoa!	*and hug baby.*

In this rhyme, the level of activity can also be modified to suit the age of the baby. For brand new babies, under three months, this is a small, gentle rhyme recited softly and slowly. As babies grow, they will enjoy much more activity and excitement in this rhyme. Make sure to remind parents to insert their own baby's name when it says "baby" in this rhyme.

Trot, Trot to Boston

Trot, trot to Boston,	*Bounce baby on knees.*
Trot, trot to Lynne.	
Look out, Baby,	
You're going to fall in!	*Lower knees on "in."*

The final lap/activity rhymes involve the adult lifting baby up. In this way, they become "flying baby" rhymes. Start off with this short traditional favorite. As soon as parents see the smile on their babies' faces, they will see the real value in flying.

Here We Go Up, Up, Up
(melody: Here We Go Looby-Loo)

Here we go up, up, up,	*Lift baby up.*
Here we go down, down, down.	*Bring baby back to lap.*
Here we go up, up, up,	*Lift baby up.*
Here we go down, down, down.	*Bring baby back to lap.*
(Get a Good Start)	

Encourage each parent to start the rhythm of this rhyme by patting their legs or their baby's legs. When it comes time for baby to go up or down, parents can lift up baby or just baby's arms.

Noble Duke of York

Oh, the noble Duke of York,
He had ten thousand men.
He marched them up
To the top of the hill,
And marched them down again.
And when they're up, they're up.
And when they're down, they're
    down.
And when they're only halfway up,
They're neither up nor down.
(*Toddlers on Parade*)

Raise baby up while
baby is riding on knees
or lift baby up in the air
and lower as words indicate.

After the action of these rhymes, follow them with these self rhymes to slow down the rhythm of the program. These are especially good rhymes for each parent to bring home after the program and use with baby on the changing table or in the tub. On the first rhyme, encourage each parent to tap baby's foot as the rhyme indicates.

Shoe the Old Horse

Shoe the old horse,
Shoe the old mare.
But let the little pony
Run bare, bare, bare.

Tap one foot.
Tap the other foot.

Tap feet together.

Diddle Diddle Dumpling

Diddle, diddle dumpling,
My son John
Went to bed
With his trousers on.
One shoe off,
And one shoe on.
Diddle, diddle dumpling,
My son, John.

"Bicycle" baby's legs or arms.

Tap each foot.

"Bicycle" baby's legs or arms.

After these quieter rhymes, the group will be settled, focused on one another and on you and ready to listen to stories. These and all of the books listed for the prewalker programs are recommended specifically for this group. Read at least one of these two books to the group. Encourage the adults to gather their babies back onto their laps and direct their babies' attention to the book.

Goodnight Moon, by Margaret Wise Brown. Illustrated by Thatcher Hurd. New York: Harper & Row, 1947. A classic goodnight book, familiar to many parents and grandparents, it's now available in board book, big book, big board book, video and kit, as well as in other languages. For the program, use a traditional edition, if for no other reason than to model to parents how well their babies will respond to this book.

Mama, Mama, by Jean Marzollo. Illustrated by Laura Regan. New York: HarperFestival, 1999. Part of the Harper Growing Tree collection, this board book is one of the few board books that can be read to a group of babies and adults successfully. Its soothing text and gentle illustrations will connect with your audience. It also makes a great lap sharing book.

Follow the read-aloud time with an opportunity for the adults to read aloud to their babies. Have enough board books ready so you can hand one to each adult. Give them time to share it with their babies. Have a few extra around, so they can have a second book if they want it. This will be a very informal time and some babies will be more interested in socializing than looking at the board book their adult is reading. Be sure to tell worried parents that it's okay. Give those adult–child pairs who are sharing a book enough time to enjoy it and when it seems like everyone is finished, follow the book time with lullabies, like the two shown here.

Star Light

Star light, star bright,
First star I see tonight,
I wish I may, I wish I might,
Have the wish I wish tonight.
(Baby Games)

Open and close straight fingers
to make "twinkles" as you sing.

Twinkle, Twinkle Little Star

Twinkle, twinkle little star,   *"Twinkle" hands in the air.*
How I wonder what you are.
Up above the world so high,
Like a diamond in the sky.
Twinkle, twinkle little star,
How I wonder what you are.
(Disney's Lullaby Album)

Encourage your group to linger for a while after the program and of course borrow the books they've shared with their babies. Use this time to make any announcements regarding books you may have that might be on display or about upcoming program dates for their babies. Finally, say or sing this final self rhyme to signal a formal end to the program.

Good-Bye Song
(melody: London Bridge)

Good-bye, good-bye,   *Time for lots of waving*
We'll see you soon,   *and blowing kisses.*
See you soon, see you soon.
Good-bye, good-bye,
We'll see you soon,
On another day.
(Toddler Tunes)

PROGRAM #2

Once again, open your program with the *Hello Song*. With returning parents and caregivers, encourage them to sing along and see how many of them join in with you the first time you sing this song.

Hello Song
(melody: London Bridge)

Hi, hello and how are you?
How are you?
How are you?
Hi, hello and how are you?
How are you today?
(*Toddler Tunes*)

Help baby to wave
throughout the song.

Begin this program with a couple of traditional Mother Goose rhymes, welcome to many with their familiar words and melodies. Parents will be happy to join in with rhymes that they recognize from their own childhood. The recorded versions of the two rhymes suggested here are just a few of many available, so try some others if these don't seem to suit your voice and personality. Invite the parents to gather their babies on their laps and join you in singing these songs.

Baa Baa Black Sheep

Baa baa black sheep,
Have you any wool?
Yes sir, yes sir,
Three bags full.

One for my master
And one for my dame.
And one for the little boy
Who lives down the lane.

(*Repeat first verse.*)
(*Toddler Tunes*)

Muffin Man

Oh, do you know the Muffin Man,
The Muffin Man, the Muffin Man?
Oh, do you know the Muffin Man,
Who lives on Drury Lane?

Oh, yes I know the Muffin Man,
The Muffin Man, the Muffin Man.
Oh, yes I know the Muffin Man.
He lives on Drury Lane.
(Ella Jenkins' Nursery Rhymes)

The action picks up with the next six songs and rhymes. First there are some clapping rhymes and songs, then some bouncing/lifting songs follow. This first song is fun to do and easy to remember. For me, the easiest way to introduce this song is to tell parents to "clap on go." The melody on the recording indicated is fun to sing along with but this song also has enough rhythm to chant it.

Baby a Go-Go

Baby a go-go,   *Bounce baby on lap*
Hey-ah!   *and clap on "go."*
Baby a go-go,
Hey-ah!
Baby a-go-ah!
Baby a go-go-go!
(The Baby Record)

Although a longer version of this next rhyme exists, this short and simple version is easiest for parents and caregivers to remember. The first time, use the phrase "Daddy comes home" throughout. The second time, change it to the phrase, "Mommy comes home." Remind parents that anybody who's not "home" for baby can be inserted into the song to comfort baby, such as older siblings in school or Grandma, who's just left.

Clap Hands, Clap Hands

Clap hands, clap hands,   *Clap hands in rhythm to the words.*
'Til Daddy comes home.
Clap hands, clap hands,
'Til Mommy comes home.

It's now time to pick up the pace of the program and use some riding and then some "flying baby" songs. The next four rhymes all incorporate a little riding and then a little jumping or flying. Start with this silly song that you sing to a familiar traditional tune. Sing the last two lines a little more quickly than the rest of the song to emphasize the humor of the words. You can say this rhyme as well.

Tommy O'Flynn
(melody: Here We Go Round the Mulberry Bush)

Tommy O'Flynn and his old gray mare   *Bounce baby on knees.*
Went off to see the country fair.
The bridge fell down,   *Lower knees.*
And the bridge fell in
And that was the end of Tommy
O'Flynn, O'Flynn, O'Flynn.   *Bounce baby* quickly *on knees.*
(The Baby Record)

This rhyme is spoken, rather than sung. Tell the parents and care-givers to bounce baby on lap or knees as you say the words. There's a "jump" at the end, so babies can get a taste of flying.

Rigadoon

Rigadoon, Rigadoon,   *Ride baby on knees or lap*
Gallop up high   *to the rhythm of the words.*
Out of the saddle
And rolling on by.

Rigadoon, rigadoon,
Now let you fly,
Sit you on mother's knee
Jump you up high.   *Lift baby on "jump."*

The action section ends with two small, but fun, flying baby rhymes as baby first jumps then bounces to "hippity, hippity, hop."

Leg over Leg

Leg over leg,
As the dog went to Dover.
When he came to a stile,
Jump!   *Lift baby up on "jump."*
He went over.

Little Frog

A little frog in a pond am I,   *Bounce baby on lap.*
Hippity, hippity, hop.
And I can jump in the air so high, *Lift baby in the air.*
Hippity, hippity, hop.   *Bounce baby on lap.*

Prewalkers are carried for such a good portion of their day (or night) that it's nice to have a song to sing while carrying baby. Ask the parents to stand up and, holding their babies in their arms, walk around the circle to this next song. They'll recognize the song, even though the words have been slightly changed to suit this baby-friendly occasion.

London Bridge

London Bridge is falling down,
Falling down, falling down.
London Bridge is falling down,
My sweet baby.

Come and take a walk around,
Walk around, walk around,
Come and take a walk around,
My sweet baby.
(*Toddler Tunes*)

Settle the group down and lead them in these self/clapping rhymes to calm things down after the activity of the riding/lifting songs and rhymes. Remind parents these rhymes are perfect to bring home and use with their babies. They are easy to remember and are perfect on the changing table or in the tub, but they can be used almost anywhere when baby is cranky, fussy, or just needs a little game when she's bored.

Catch a Wee Mouse

Round about, round about,   *Trace circle on baby's back, hand or*
Catch a wee mouse.   *belly.*
Up at bit, up a bit,   *Walk fingers up to baby's chin.*
In a wee house.   *Tickle baby under chin.*

Round About

Round about, round about   *Circle baby's palm, back, or belly*
Sat a little hare.   *with finger.*
The puppies came and chased him *Run fingers up arm, back, or belly.*
Right up there!   *Tickle under chin.*

It's time for books to be read aloud to the group. Ask parents and care-givers to gather their babies in their laps so they can point out the book to the babies in order to gently encourage them to listen to the book.

Where Does the Brown Bear Go? by Nicki Weiss. New York: Green-willow, 1989. This book's soothing, repetitive text and simple, bright fig-ures on black backgrounds make this a wonderful choice both for a group and lap-time sharing.

Bounce, Bounce, Bounce, by Kathy Henderson. Illustrated by Carol Thompson. Cambridge, MA: Candlewick Press, 1994. Called a lap game in a book, this, along with a similar title by Henderson, *Bumpety, Bump,* will encourage interactions between parent and child and embraces the joy of babyhood.

Use the time following the read-aloud to allow grownups and babies to share books together, and make sure to have plenty of board books on hand to give to the grownups. When the informal reading time is over, ask your parents to gather their babies back into their laps and follow with these two lullabies.

See Saw Margery Daw

See saw Margery Daw.
Baby loves when we hug her.
Baby has all the hugs in the world.
Because she knows we love her.

Rock-a-Bye Baby

Rock-a-bye baby,
In the tree top.
When the winds blow,
The cradle will rock.
When the bough breaks,
The cradle will fall.
And down will come baby,
Cradle and all.
(*Nursery Rhyme Time*)

*A great song for hugging
and rocking.*

The attention of your group will be at its best at this moment, because the lullabies act as both a calming and a unifying element. Take advantage of this time to make announcements about the next program's day and time, any books that you may want your group to know about and borrow, and to thank them for coming to the program. Following your announcements, sing your good-bye song.

Good-Bye Song
(melody: London Bridge)

Good-bye, good-bye,
We'll see you soon,
See you soon, see you soon.
Good-bye, good-bye,
We'll see you soon,
On another day.
(*Toddler Tunes*)

*Time for lots of waving
and blowing kisses.*

PROGRAM #3

Hello Song
(melody: London Bridge)

Hi, hello and how are you?
How are you?
How are you?
Hi, hello and how are you?
How are you today?
(*Toddler Tunes*)

*Help baby to wave
throughout the song.*

Many of the songs that follow are classic Mother Goose rhymes. Some young parents may know them but others will be hearing them for the first time. The first two songs are somewhat less familiar, but still traditional Mother Goose rhymes, set to songs most parents will know. When used with familiar tunes as they are here, they can become fun, rousing songs, sure to make everyone feel comfortable. Tell your parents to bounce their babies gently on their laps in time to the melody. The first song is a variation on a traditional rhyme, with special "prewalker" lyrics.

Baby Dear, Come Out to Play
(melody: Baa Baa Black Sheep)

Baby dear, come out to play,
The sun is shining this bright day.
Bring your mommy and daddy too.
Here's all these babies to play with you.
Baby dear, come out to play,
The sun is shining this bright day.
(*Toddler Tunes*)

Alley-Oh
(melody: The Muffin Man)

The big ship sails on the alley alley-oh,
The alley alley-oh, the alley alley-oh,
The big ship sails on the alley alley-oh
On this fine day in September.   *Substitute whatever month is*
(*Toddler Tunes*)   *appropriate.*

Follow these songs with another more familiar tune that calls for lots of rocking baby on lap to the rhythm and tune of the song.

Hey Diddle Diddle

Hey diddle, diddle,
The cat and the fiddle,
The cow jumped over the moon.
The little dog laughed to see such fun,
And the dish ran away with the spoon.
(*Ella Jenkins' Nursery Rhymes*)

Although many babies cannot clap on their own at this age, encourage parents to clap for their babies, either clapping their own hands in front of the babies or help them to clap. Similarly, although babies clearly cannot count, if done often enough, they'll soon recognize the words and the rhyme scheme will work to help them anticipate what comes next in this classic rhyme which will be familiar to so many parents.

One, Two, Buckle My Shoe

One, two, buckle my shoe.	*Clap twice, tap shoes.*
Three, four, shut the door.	*Clap twice, clap hands.*
Five, six, pick up sticks.	*Clap hands, wiggle fingers.*
Seven, eight, lay them straight.	*Clap hands, pat hands on floor.*
Nine, ten, a big fat hen.	*Clap hands, widen arms.*

Now for some riding/flying songs. A less familiar rhyme is set to the familiar tune of *Here We Go Round the Mulberry Bush.* Tell parents to ride their babies on their knees or laps for a fun ride on their own personal merry-go-round. For an active version of this song, turn it into a circle game, by asking your parents to stand and carry their babies around the circle as they sing this song. There will be plenty of times they'll have to calm fussy babies by carrying them around the house. You may as well give them a good song to use for those stressful times.

Riding the Merry-go-Round
(melody: Here We Go Round the Mulberry Bush)

Take a ride on the merry-go-round,
Around and around
Around and around
The horses go up and the horses go down,
Around and around and around.
(*Ella Jenkins' Nursery Rhymes*)

A bit of humor can be built into this lap-riding rhyme. Stretch out the word "off" each time it's said. Then, on the last line, say "on and on and on" a bit faster, even repeating this phrase.

Mother and Father and Uncle John

Mother and Father and Uncle John   *Bounce baby on knee.*
Went to town, one by one.
Mother jumped off.   *Lean to one side.*
Father jumped off.   *Lean to other side.*
But Uncle John went on and on and on. *Bounce baby on knee.*

Two spoken rhymes follow that give each parent an opportunity to lift baby up and let her "fly." In this first little rhyme, the phrase "and away she goes" is the parent's cue to lift baby off knee for a bit of flying.

Rooster Crows

One, two, three,
Baby's on my knee.
Rooster crows
And away he goes.   *Lift baby up.*

The second rhyme is a special prewalker variation on a familiar rhyme. The small story it tells is filled with drama, suspense, and a happy ending. Put as much drama in it as you can. Parents who may be reluctant to do this will soon join in when they see big smiles on the other babies as they are plucked from the apple tree.

Away up High

Away up high in the apple tree.   *Lift baby up.*
I saw a little baby smiling at me.
I shook that tree as hard as I could.   *Shake baby gently.*
Down came the baby.   *Bring baby down for a hug.*
Mmm, was she good!   *Give baby a kiss.*

Now for some smaller, quieter rhymes that concentrate on touching baby. Since it's always good to start with the familiar, this rhyme should be a favorite with many parents. Encourage them to rub their baby's back, belly, or bottom and, of course, to use this rhyme at home in baby's own tub.

Rub a Dub Dub

Rub a dub dub,	*Rub baby's back or belly.*
Three men in a tub,	
And who do you think they be?	
The butcher, the baker,	*Clap three times.*
The candlestick maker,	
Throw 'em out,	*Lean back with baby and hug baby.*
Knaves, all three!	

Another couple of small rhymes can be used on the changing table, tub, or playpen at home. The first invites circles to be drawn on baby's belly, then the parent's fingers walk up baby's belly for a tickle under the chin. The second rhyme is a great one for bare feet: feet that love to be tickled, patted, and kissed. Before you do the rhyme the first time, describe the actions parents will do.

Round and Round the Garden

Round and round the garden	*Trace circle on belly or back.*
Goes the teddy bear.	
One step, two step,	*Walk fingers up belly or back.*
Tickle under there.	*Tickle under chin.*

Pitty Patty Polt

Pitty patty polt,	*Tap baby's feet together.*
Shoe the little colt,	
Here a nail,	*Tap one foot.*
There a nail,	*Tap the other foot.*
Pitty, patty, polt.	*Tap baby's feet together.*

After these quiet rhymes, read a book or two to the group. Two books are suggested, even though you may only be able to read one successfully, depending on the activity and attention of the group that day.

Time for Bed, by Mem Fox. Illustrated by Jane Dyer. San Diego: Harcourt, Brace, Jovanovich, 1993. All sorts of animal babies and mothers repeat the phrase that is the title, as they tuck their little ones in, coaxing them to sleep. Lush illustrations add to the mood of this lovely book that is available in board book and big book.

Baby! Talk! by Penny Gentieu. New York: Crown Publishers, 1999. Short on text, but long on photos of adorable babies doing all sorts of adorable things that baby will recognize, like "Peek-a-Boo."

After you read these books to the group, give the grownups in your group the opportunity to read to their own babies. Hand each grownup in the group a board book they can read to their baby and keep a couple extra, in case they need a second book. This informal time in your program gives everyone an opportunity to enjoy their babies and it gives the babies an opportunity to cuddle with their grownups and to socialize a bit with their neighbors.

After the quiet of the read-aloud time and the socializing of the reading together time, invite all the parents and caregivers to gather their babies back onto their laps for a couple of lullabies.

Bye Low, My Baby

Bye low, my baby.
Bye low, my baby, bye.
Bye low, my baby.
Rock-a-baby, bye.
(From Wibbleton to Wobbleton)

Hush-a-Bye

Hush-a-bye, don't you cry.
Go to sleepy, little baby.
When you wake, you shall have
All the pretty little horses.
Blacks and bays, dapples and grays,
All the pretty little horses.
Hush-a-bye, don't you cry.
Go to sleepy, little baby.
(Lullaby, a Collection)

After lullabies, spend a moment or two reminding parents of the upcoming events in the library, including the next program. You can also take this time to remind parents to take a book or two home, especially the ones they've been sharing with their babies. Always sing your good-bye song.

Good-Bye Song
(melody: London Bridge)

Good-bye, good-bye,
We'll see you soon,
See you soon, see you soon.
Good-bye, good-bye,
We'll see you soon,
On another day.
(Toddler Tunes)

Time for lots of waving
and blowing kisses.

PROGRAM #4

Hello Song
(melody: London Bridge)

Hi, hello and how are you?
How are you?
How are you?
Hi, hello and how are you?
How are you today?
(Toddler Tunes)

Help baby to wave
throughout the song.

This fun, fast-paced chant is repeated here. Remember to instruct caregivers to gently lift up babies' arms, but only if their babies will permit it.

Exercises, Exercises

Exercises, exercises
Let's all do our exercises.
Exercises, exercises
Let's all do our exercises.

Lift baby's arms gently
in the air to the rhythm
of this rhyme.

This song, used at this point in Program #1, is also repeated here. Its bouncing melody, clapping, and bouncing of baby will bring everybody into the program. Its familiar melody will encourage parents and caregivers to join in. On the second time through, they'll be able to sing along.

Say, Say, Oh Baby

Say, say, oh baby,
Come here and clap with me.   *Hold baby on lap*
And bring your happy smile,   *and do what the song*
Bounce on my lap so free.   *tells you to do.*
Shake, shake your hands, now.
Shake, shake your bottom too.
And shake your tootsies ten.
Let's do it again.
(*Baby Games*)

This song will usually produce a chuckle from moms and caregivers all too familiar with babies who won't sleep when their parents wish they would. This is a lively song that has a rich history in American folklore and is still perfect for gently bouncing baby on your lap. You can add as many verses as you want and a few are suggested here.

What'll We Do with the Baby-O?

What'll we do with the baby-o?
What'll we do with the baby-o?
What'll we do with the baby-o?
When she won't go to sleepy-o.

Wrap her up in calico.
Wrap her up in calico.
Wrap her up in calico.
And send her to her mommy-o.
(*Repeat chorus.*)

Dance her north and dance her south.
Dance her north and dance her south.
Dance her north and dance her south.
And put a little honey in her mouth.
(*Repeat chorus.*)
(*Tickles & Tunes*)

These next two clapping rhymes will continue the lively rhythm of the program set by the first two songs, as parents will clap along with these rhymes and will set the stage for the riding rhymes to follow. The second time you sing the first song, have parents and caregivers insert the names of their own babies instead of using the word "baby."

Clap Your Hands

Clap your hands, little baby,
Clap your hands, little baby, dear,
Clap your hands, little baby,
Clap 'em, Baby dear.
(The Baby Record)

Pease Porridge Hot

Pease porridge hot,   *Clap hands in rhythm to the words.*
Pease porridge cold.
Pease porridge in the pot,
Nine days old.
Some like it hot, some like it cold.
Some like it in the pot,
Nine days old.

It's time for some riding rhymes and songs. Use this first rhyme in two ways. You can invite parents to set their babies on their knees or get the group up and walking around in a circle, holding their babies, as they go "round the sun."

Baby, Go Round the Sun

Baby, go round the sun,   *Parents walk around the circle,*
Baby, go round the moon.   *holding their babies or*
Baby, go round the circle,   *parents set babies on their knees*
On a sunny afternoon.   *and have them ride to the song.*
(Get a Good Start)

Once the group is settled back down on the floor, ask the caregivers and parents to put their babies on their knees, as long as the babies are old enough to sit up on their own. They can face their parents or the rest of the group. For very young babies, tell parents to cradle their babies gently on their laps as they use these rhymes.

You can sing or chant the first riding song. Its strong rhythm will work with or without music. Model to parents the way they can touch their babies' fingers or toes as these words are used in the rhyme.

Ride a Cock Horse

Ride a cock horse
To Banbury Cross.
To see a fine lady
Upon a white horse.

With rings on her fingers
And bells on her toes.
She shall have music
Wherever she goes.
(*Hap Palmer Sings Classic Nursery Rhymes*)

Build lots of humor into this next rhyme as you emphasize the different rides your baby will get with the farmer, the lady, and the gentleman. As you demonstrate each of the different ways baby can ride, say the words slowly and speed up on the phrase, "Gallop, gallop, gallop." One thing is for sure: baby will love the "gallop."

This Is the Way the Farmer Rides

This is the way the farmer rides,
A-jiggity jog, a jiggity jog.   *Rock baby side to side on knees.*
The is the way the lady rides.
A-prance, a-prance.   *Bounce baby gently on knees.*
This is the way the gentleman rides,
A gallop, gallop, gallop!   *Bounce baby quickly on knees.*

This next rhyme involves both a little knee-riding and some flying as baby is lifted high over the parent's head. This will produce lots of giggles and smiles all around.

Flying Man

Flying man, flying man,   *Bounce baby on lap.*
Up in the sky,   *Lift baby up.*
Where are you going to,   *Bounce baby on lap.*
Flying so high?

Flying man, flying man,   *Bounce baby on lap.*
Over the sea,   *Lift baby up.*
Flying man, flying man,   *Bounce baby on lap.*
Please take me!   *Hug baby.*

This next very familiar rhyme has the kind of drama any good story should have. As you chant this rhyme, parents can lift their babies up on the word "up" in this rhyme or simply bounce the babies on their knees to the rhythm of the tune.

Jack and Jill

Jack and Jill went up the hill,   *Ride baby on knees in rhythm to the*
To fetch a pail of water.   *rhyme.*
Jack fell down and broke his crown.
And Jill came tumbling after.

Some self/clapping rhymes can now calm things down after the energy of riding and flying and will get your group ready for stories. Remind the parents that these are perfect to take home and use with their babies when they are in the bath or on the changing table.

This Little Pig

This little pig went to market,   *Touch baby's fingers or toes, one by*
This little pig stayed home.   *one.*
This little pig had roast beef.
This little pig had none.
This little pig cried,
"Wee, wee, wee," all the way home.   *Run fingers up baby's arm or leg.*

Before doing these two rhymes, describe the way parents should trace a circle on their babies and then walk fingers up to babies' chins for a tickle.

Round About

Round about, round about,   *Circle baby's palm, back, or belly*
Sat a little hare.   *with finger.*
The puppies came and chased him   *Run fingers up arm, back, or belly.*
Right up there!   *Tickle under chin.*

Round and Round the Garden

Round and round the garden,	Circle baby's palm, back, or belly.
Goes the teddy bear.	
One step, two step,	Walk fingers up arm, back, or chest.
Tickle under there.	Tickle under chin.

With the babies calmed down and attentive, it's time for stories. These two books focus on babies, celebrating who they are and what they can do. Both are board books, but in this kind of intimate program, they work very well to connect to baby.

Baby Dance, by Ann Taylor. Illustrated by Marie Van Heerden. Harper Growing Tree. New York: HarperFestival, 1999. Father and baby dance to a lilting poem as they swing up and down, around and around.

Show Me! by Tom Tracy. Illustrated by Darica LaBrosse. Harper Growing Tree. New York: HarperFestival, 1999. Parents celebrate baby's nose, cheek, tummy, etc. All ends in a hug.

Distribute board books to the parents so they can share books with their babies. Each parent–child pair will find its own way of sharing, with some babies more attentive than others. Try to communicate to parents that whatever makes their babies comfortable is the best method for them, so parents should never feel obligated to hold their babies on their laps if they don't want to be there. After giving everyone enough time for both reading and socializing, ask parents to gather their babies onto their laps and close the books they've been reading to sing some lullabies.

Although few people still go to the mail boat, the small story this tells of Daddy, then Mommy, going away and coming back is a tale all babies understand. This is longer than most of the lullabies suggested here, but its soft, soothing lullaby will entice parents to join you on the second verse.

Go to Sleepy, Baby-Bye

Go to sleepy, baby-bye.
Go to sleepy, baby-bye.
Daddy's gone to the mail boat.
Daddy's gone to the mail boat,
Bye.

Bye-low, baby, bye,
Bye-low, baby, bye,
Mommy's gone to the mail boat.
Mommy's gone to the mail boat,
Bye.
(*From Wibbleton to Wobbleton*)

Lavender's Blue

Lavender's blue, dilly, dilly.
Lavender's green.
When I am king, dilly dilly,
You shall be queen.

Who told you so, dilly dilly,
Who told you so.
'Twas my own heart, dilly, dilly,
That told me so.
(*KidSongs 2*)

At this time, make announcements about upcoming programs and encourage your parents to bring home books to read to their babies. Before you sing your good-bye song, take the time to again thank the parents, grandparents, and other caregivers for coming and sharing this important time with their babies. Babyhood is a special but elusive time, the more they sing and the more language they share, the more enriched their babies will become.

Good-Bye Song
(melody: London Bridge)

Good-bye, good-bye,   *Time for lots of waving*
We'll see you soon,   *and blowing kisses.*
See you soon, see you soon.
Good-bye, good-bye,
We'll see you soon,
On another day.
(Toddler Tunes)

PROGRAM #5

Hello Song
(melody: London Bridge)

Hi, hello and how are you?
How are you?   *Help baby to wave*
How are you?   *throughout the song.*
Hi, hello and how are you?
How are you today?
(Toddler Tunes)

Well-known Mother Goose rhymes are always welcome at the beginning of a program. Returning parents as well as newcomers will
feel comfortable in singing along with you on this first song. The second rhyme, which is spoken, has great rhythm, lots of silly sounds,
and plenty of repetition. For both of these rhymes, tell parents to
hold their babies on their laps and bounce them gently to the rhythm
of the songs.

Muffin Man

Oh, do you know the Muffin Man,
The Muffin Man, the Muffin Man?
Oh, do you know the Muffin Man,
Who lives on Drury Lane?

Oh, yes, I know the Muffin Man,
The Muffin Man, the Muffin Man.
Oh, yes, I know the Muffin Man,
He lives on Drury Lane.
(*Ella Jenkins' Nursery Rhymes*)

From Wibbleton to Wobbleton

From Wibbleton to Wobbleton is   *Rock baby from side to side.*
 fifteen miles.
From Wobbleton to Wibbleton is
 fifteen miles.
Wibbleton to Wobbleton,
Wobbleton to Wibbleton,
From Wibbleton to Wobbleton is
 fifteen miles.

Use some clapping rhymes here to pick up the rhythm of the program. The first rhyme can be used with all ages. Although most prewalkers really can't clap, it's never too early to start teaching this classic rhyme to babies. For the most part, they love to watch their parents and caregivers clap, pat, roll, and mark with a B.

Pat-a-Cake

Pat-a-cake, pat-a-cake,   *Clap hands in rhythm to the words.*
Baker's man.
Bake me a cake
As fast as you can.

Roll it and pat it,   *Roll hands, pat hands together.*
And mark it with a B.   *Trace B on baby's hand.*
And put it in the oven,
For baby and me!   *Point to baby and self.*

This clapping rhyme is a traditional Mother Goose rhyme with a combination of silly words, nonsense rhymes, and familiar words that grownups will laugh at and babies will love to listen to.

Handy Spandy

Handy, spandy, sugardy candy,   *Clap in rhythm to the words.*
French, almond rock.
Bread and butter's   *Say words and clap more quickly here.*
For your supper's
All your mother's got!

Ask each parent and caregiver to roll their own hands in front of baby, or if baby will let them, ask them to roll baby's hands. This is also a great rhyme for the parent to trace a circle on baby's belly. This rhyme is so short, you'll want to do it several times. Say the first two lines slowly and quicken the pace on the second two lines.

Roly Poly

Roly poly,   *Roll hands slowly.*
Ever so slowly
Roly poly,   *Roll hands faster and faster.*
Faster, faster, faster.

Although this is a great lap-riding song, you can use this song as a carrying song, as well. Ask parents to stand and walk around the circle until the "whoas" of the song. On that line, everyone stops and hugs baby. If you do this as a lap-riding song, parents lean babies back for a hug on "whoa."

Riding on My Pony

Riding on my pony,   *Carry baby or ride on knees.*
My pony, my pony.
Riding on my pony,
Whoa, whoa, whoa.   *Hug baby.*
(*From Wibbleton to Wobbleton*)

Continue the walking with baby with this next song, in which letters and numbers are used to make the rhyme and the question asked of baby is one every parent asks. And the question can be changed to many things like sleep or burp or whatever the parent is hoping baby will do.

One, Two, Three, Four, Five

One, two, three, four, five,   *Carry baby or ride on knees.*
My little baby pie,
A,B,C,D,E,F,G,
Would you like to smile for me?
(*Wibbleton to Wobbleton*)

These two lap-riding songs also can be two flying-baby songs. The first, a traditional rhyme, is spoken. It's a small rhyme that introduces the idea of lifting baby up in the air. Tell parents to lift baby up on the word "over." They can also sit baby on one side of their legs and, on the word, "over," lift baby to the other side. The babies will be delighted and the parents will love the smiles they get from their little ones.

Jack Be Nimble

Jack be nimble,   *Bounce baby on knees.*
Jack be quick.
Jack jump over   *Lift baby up on "over."*
The candlestick.

The second rhyme is often sung, but it can be done as a spoken rhyme as well. If parents feel strong enough, they can lift the babies up and down on the appropriate lines, ride them up and down on their knees, or even just lift up and lower babies' arms. Tell the parents to pat out the rhythm on their own knees or their babies' legs to begin the rhyme.

Noble Duke of York

Oh, the noble Duke of York,
He had ten thousand men,
He marched them up   *Raise baby.*
To the top of the hill,
And marched them down again.   *Lower baby.*

And when they're up, they're up,   *Raise baby.*
And when they're down, they're down, *Lower baby.*
And when they're only halfway up,   *Raise baby halfway.*
They're neither up nor down.   *Raise then lower baby.*
(*Where is Thumbkin?*)

Smaller, quieter rhymes that concentrate on the grownup patting baby's belly are a nice change after the excitement and activity of riding and flying. So here are some rhymes that work well in the program or at home on the changing table or tub. On most of these rhymes, remind parents to trace a circle wherever baby will let them, whether it's belly, back, or bottom. On this first rhyme, parents really should circle baby's belly. After all, the belly is the butter dish!

Round and Round the Butter Dish

Round and round the butter dish,   *Circle baby's belly.*
One, two, three,   *Tap baby gently three times.*
A little here, a little there,   *Tickle each cheek.*
As tasty as can be.   *Tickle baby's tummy gently.*

Round and Round the Haystack

Round and round the haystack,   *Trace a circle on baby's belly or back.*
Goes the little mousie.
One step, two step,   *Walk fingers up baby's chest.*
In his little housie.   *Tickle gently behind baby's ear.*

This next rhyme is a perfect rhyme for parents to bring home and use in so many situations. Remind parents, although you probably won't need to, that the second time through they should use their own babies' names instead of "baby."

These are Baby's Fingers

These are baby's fingers.	*Gently touch baby's fingers.*
These are baby's toes.	*Gently touch baby's toes.*
This is baby's belly button.	*Point to baby's belly button.*
Round and round it goes.	*Trace a circle on baby's belly.*

A shorter version of the more familiar tub rhyme, this quick rhyme invites parents to insert their own babies' names as they answer the question, "Who's in the tub?" Model this for parents, using a name from the group.

Rub a Dub Dub, Who's in the Tub?

Rub a dub dub,
Who's in the tub?
Little baby (name)
Scrub, scrub, scrub.

After these quiet, intimate rhymes, it's time for reading aloud to the group. Invite parents to settle their babies onto their laps while you read one or both of these books.

Baby's Boat, by Jeanne Titherington. New York: Greenwillow, 1992. Using the words to a classic lullaby that is also known as "Baby's Bed," this book brings these words to life, using gentle, lavender-hued illustrations and the placement of one or two lines per page to keep the words flowing. The music for the lullaby is also included.

You Are My Perfect Baby, by Joyce Carol Thomas. Illustrated by Nineka Bennet. Harper Growing Tree. New York: HarperFestival, 1999. An ode of love from mother to baby as everything on baby, from nose to toes, is exclaimed over with joy. Another board book that works well in a group.

After the relative formality of reading aloud to this group, allow some time for grownups and babies to share books together. Give each caregiver a board book to share with or read to their baby. Some babies will be happy to have another book read to them, but others may be more interested in socializing. So, this will be a relaxed, informal time for both reading and chatting. After several minutes, ask the parents and caregivers to gather their babies back onto their laps and sing a lullaby or two. These two lullabies have a history and heritage deep in the tradition of American and British folklore. They are odes from loving parent to adored baby.

Dance to Your Daddy
(melody: Twinkle Twinkle)

Dance to your daddy,
My little baby,
Dance to your daddy,
My little lamb.

You shall have a fishy
In a little dishy,
You shall have a fishy
When the boat comes in.

(Repeat first verse.)
(Get a Good Start)

Hush-a-Bye

Hush-a-bye,
Don't you cry.
Go to sleepy, little baby.
When you wake, you shall have
All the pretty little horses.

Blacks and bays,
Dapples and grays,
All the pretty little horses.

(Repeat first verse.)
(Sleepy Times Rock-a-byes)

The group will be quiet and calm after the lullabies, so take that opportunity to make any announcements you may have. The most important one is the reminder to all to sing, say rhymes, and read to their babies at home and continue the wonderful experiences they've had at the library. End with the *Good-Bye Song.*

Good-Bye Song
(melody: London Bridge)

Good-bye, good-bye,
We'll see you soon,
See you soon, see you soon.
Good-bye, good-bye,
We'll see you soon,
On another day.
(*Toddler Tunes*)

*Time for lots of waving
and blowing kisses.*

❸

WALKER PROGRAMS

WHAT WORKS FOR WALKERS

Babies who are walking, usually ranging in age from fourteen or fifteen months to two or two and a half years old, are lively and active little ones who want to be entertained with an almost nonstop mix of songs, rhymes, circle games, books, and even a puppet or two. They are constantly changing: they are beginning to notice the other babies, grownups other than their parents, and the world around them. Their mood and even their enjoyment in a song, rhyme, or book may also change from program to program or even one moment to the next. So be prepared for this spirited and mercurial group with a program that will keep them and their caregivers happy.

The walker rhymes included in this book are divided into several categories. There are clapping/finger rhymes, pretend rhymes, and action songs. Clapping/finger rhymes include such classic and traditional rhymes such as *Patty Cake* or *Pease Porridge Hot* and other clapping and finger rhymes that help little ones practice those newfound clapping skills. Pretend rhymes cover a wide range of subjects, such as food, with *I Eat My Peas with Honey,* weather with the ever-popular *Mr. Sun* and classic Mother Goose rhymes, such as *Humpty Dumpty* or *Jack and Jill.*

Action songs are clearly the specialty for walkers, with such full body rhymes and songs such as *Head, Shoulders, Knees and Toes, I'm a Little Teapot,* and *Ring Around the Rosie.* The walker rhymes are much livelier than the prewalker rhymes, matching the higher level of activity that walkers exhibit. Of course, they will also enjoy many of the songs and rhymes classified here as for prewalkers. But in a group setting, the walker rhymes included here will yield a much higher success rate.

THE FRAMEWORK OF THE PROGRAM

This program continues the philosophy of language enrichment started in the prewalker programs. It expands the scope of the program beyond just baby into the world around him, both real and pretend. It reinforces such skills as clapping, standing, walking, and sharing. It is as interactive as the baby wants to be, since participation is by no means required, but always welcome. Some babies will sing and clap and smile while others will just sit and stare. But don't be fooled by the solemn babies who can only stare at you. They are listening just as hard as the babies who are clapping and singing. A program for walkers can last slightly longer than prewalkers programs, perhaps twenty-five to thirty minutes. Some of the songs included will be long, depending on the number of verses included, and there is more movement, which always takes up more time. But as with prewalkers, the right mix of clapping rhymes, pretend rhymes, and action songs will lead to success.

Welcome both baby and grownup as they arrive in your children's room or library. They will be tentative if they are new, so make sure they know where the program will take place and where they should go until it starts. It's always a good idea to have board books around for baby and grownup to share until the formal beginning of the program. Although walkers will be eager to play with the library's toys or puzzles, especially if they are regular patrons and know they are there, it's not a good idea to have toys or puzzles out, since that will lead to a mess you'll need to clean up before you can start.

When you are ready to begin, make sure that food and personal toys are put away and ask everyone to sit down and form a circle on the floor. If you have older adults, a few stools might be necessary for their comfort.

Once everyone is comfortably settled into a circle on the floor, introduce yourself and your program. Welcome everyone and briefly describe the program as an opportunity to share rhymes, songs, and books
in order to enrich their babies' language and listening skills. Thank the
parents who've come to your program and remind them that babies do
not always want to sit and listen and that if baby does not want to stay
for the entire program, it's best to take him or her out. Sometimes babies will only last through one-third or half a program. It's okay if they
can't last the whole time. Maybe next time, they'll do better.

A baby who does not want to stay is different from a baby who does
not want to sit, however. Remind parents of restless children that a baby
wandering around in the middle or the outside of the circle is fine. As
long as he doesn't distract anybody else, that baby's still listening and enjoying the program.

It's best to open your program with the same rhyme each time to establish a sense of continuity and to enhance their recognition of the program.
Here, the same rhyme that was used to start your prewalker programs is
used to open this program. With this group, however, it will involve more
activity, since most of the babies will be able to wave on their own. They
may not all be willing at first, but they will, once they get to know you. As
always, sing it twice. After the *Hello Song*, the content of each of the programs included here is different, although the format is similar. A longer,
warmup song always follows the *Hello Song*. That gives you a chance to get
settled into the program and your babies and grownups can get settled and
feel comfortable as well. Since this song is rather long, just sing three or
four verses through once. Don't try to repeat any of it.

When the song is available on a recording, the name of one recording
is listed below the rhyme. The full citation for the recording will appear
in the bibliography in the back. If the song in the program uses different words to a traditional tune, as happens in Program #1, for example,
when *Clap, Clap, Clap Your Hands* is sung to the tune of *Row, Row,
Row Your Boat*, the recording listed below the rhyme will have the
words to the original song. It is listed in this way to help you become familiar with the tune or if you just need to hear it before you sing it. With
many of the songs, the recordings listed will have both the melody and
the words that are being used in the program, giving you the option to
use the tape or CD in the program. That takes practice, however, so try

it a couple of times before you use a CD or tape in your program. One or two of the recordings cited here have one track with the words and music for a song and a second track with just the music. They can be particularly helpful if you're singing a traditional song with different words. It's also helpful to announce that a particular song is sung to the tune of *Row, Row, Row Your Boat,* for example, so parents will be able to jump in and sing with you from almost the beginning of the song.

A few clapping rhymes and songs will follow, which continues your warm-up, with a mixture of familiar and new songs and rhymes. Pretend rhymes are next in the walker format, and hopefully, by this time in the program, everyone will feel more comfortable and ready to play a bit with you. A wide variety of pretend rhymes are contained in these programs, from food rhymes that are great to use around the house and rhymes and songs that celebrate weather and nature that can go out to the playground or yard or for a walk. Rhymes and songs make life more fun so the more rhymes and songs that babies and their grownups can incorporate into their everyday lives, the more fun they will have and the more that both baby and parent will learn.

A segment particular to the walkers are activity rhymes that always invite baby and adult to stand up and use their whole bodies in the rhyme. Many of these are circle games, like *Ring Around the Rosie* or *Here we Go Round the Mulberry Bush.* Since babies at this age are only beginning to participate in group activities, be aware that circle games involve a bit of a risk for you. There will be babies who won't want to do this activity. So, before you begin a circle game activity, be sure to advise parents and caregivers that their little one might not want to join in right away. He or she might insist on being carried and just plant him or herself on the floor and refuse to get up. Once in a while a baby might cry, slightly panicked by the sight of everyone else standing up. Please make it clear to the parent that it's okay if their baby does not want to join in. Or if they need to be carried, carry them. Insisting that a reluctant baby walk or join in when she doesn't want to will lead to more tears and frustration. Just as flexibility should be your hallmark, encourage the parents to be flexible too. As long as everyone is happy, the activity will succeed.

Each program contains about four of these activity and/or circle game rhymes. After the action is over and everyone is settled, it's time for stories and, if you like to use them, you can introduce a small puppet or finger puppet at this time.

Introducing a finger puppet into the program accomplishes several things. It shifts the focus of the group onto the puppet. It gives the babies, if they want it, an opportunity to come up and touch the puppet, wave to it, blow kisses, whatever is comfortable. You can also say a rhyme or sing a song about the puppet and there is one included in each program. Many of them are also rhymes or songs that parent and baby can use on their walks or rides outside. Finally, this puppet gives the program a nice break from its structure and, as long as the puppet disappears back into the bag or box from which it appeared, the group will be happy to focus on the books that come next.

Two books are suggested for each walker program and there are additional titles suggested in the bibliography. They may or may not have anything to do with the rhymes or puppet that was in the program but they will all have bright, colorful illustrations and lilting, usually rhyming text that tells a story that walkers can relate to and understand.

You may, as you did with the prewalkers, give everyone a book to read with their babies after you've done your own read aloud. This will work as well with the walkers as it did with the prewalkers and many groups will have babies who look forward to having their own book in their hands to share with their grownups.

ENDING THE PROGRAM

A few closing rhymes are suggested after the book time. They are a few finger and clapping rhymes, maybe a round of *Ring Around the Rosie* and, of course, your *Good-Bye Song*. Before your *Good-Bye Song*, make any closing announcements you may wish to and always thank your adults for attending this very important program and making listening, learning, and language an important part of their children's day.

It can never be repeated too many times that they are starting their children off on the path to listening, learning, and reading. The rich language, the new words, the lively songs, and the bright and colorful books are all keys contained in this program that will lead to the treasure of reading that your baby will enjoy and continue to enjoy as he grows. So join us in this wonderful world that brings babies into your library.

WALKERS RHYME LIST

Pretend Rhymes
Baa Baa Black Sheep
Brush Hair, Brush
Five Little Robins
Flower Play
Good-Bye Song
Green Leaf
Hello Song
Here Is a Doughnut
Here Is the Beehive
Here We Go Round the
  Mulberry Bush
Here's a Cup
Higglety Pigglety Pop
Hot Cross Buns
Humpty Dumpty
I Saw a Little Rabbit
Jack and Jill
Little Boy Blue
Little Brown Seed
Little Leaves
Little Miss Muffet
Mary Had a Little Lamb
Pitter Patter
Polly Put the Kettle On
Rain on the Rooftops
Rain/Shine Song
Ten Little Gentlemen
The Wheels on the Bus
This Is My Garden
This Little Pig
Wash the Dishes

Action Rhymes
Bend and Stretch
Down by the Station
Exercises, Exercises

I'm a Little Teapot
I Put My Arms up High
Jump, Jump
Head, Shoulders, Knees
  and Toes
Hickory Dickory Dock
Marching Song
Mister Sun
Ring around the Rosie
Teddy Bear
The Big Ship
These Are Baby's Fingers
Two by Two
Up, Up, Up

Clapping Rhymes
Clap, Clap, Clap Your Hands
Come a Look a See
Fee, Fi, Fo, Fum
I Clap My Hands
I Eat My Peas with Honey
I Have Ten Fingers
I Wiggle My Fingers
If You're Happy and You
  Know It
One, Two, Buckle My Shoe
Open, Shut Them
Pat-a-Cake
Pease Porridge Hot
Put Your Finger on Your Shirt
Right Hand, Left Hand
Roll, Roll, Roll Your Hands
Sing with Me
They're a Part of Me
Where is Thumbkin?
Wiggle, Wiggle Fingers
With Our Hands

Puppet Rhymes
Baby Bumble Bee
The Bee
Birds in a Nest
Bluebird, Bluebird
Bunny in Hat
Bunny Rhyme
Five Kittens in the Bed
Five Little Monkeys
Flowers
Four Flowers in a Pot
Frog

Little Frog
Mouse in Cheese
Puppies in Basket
Redbirds
The Itsy-Bitsy Spider
The Squirrel
Three Bunnies
Three Chicks
Three Pigs
Three Puppies Song
Three White Mice in a Red Box
Turtle

WALKER PROGRAM #1

Hello Song
(melody: London Bridge)

Hi, hello and how are you?   *Adults and babies wave hello.*
How are you? How are you?
Hi, hello and how are you?
How are you today?
(*Toddler Tunes*)

Start your program with a long song that involves some kind of activity like clapping or tapping or stretching. Follow that with some short, simple clapping rhymes and songs. This part of your program is your warmup, so don't put too many expectations on your group. Let everyone get comfortable with you and the program. A song with lots of verses will give everyone an opportunity to join in when they're ready. This song, sung to the tune of *Row, Row, Row Your Boat*, is a great warmup song. It's filled with a lot of simple activity, using a tune most grownups know.

Clap, Clap, Clap Your Hands
(melody: Row, Row, Row Your Boat)

Clap, clap, clap your hands.
Clap them now with me.
Clap your hands, let me see,
Clap them now with me.

(Do as many verses as you like)

Tap, tap, tap your knees.
Shake, shake, shake your feet.
Touch, touch, touch your shoulders.
(Songs & Games for Toddlers)

Once your group is warmed up and everyone is fairly attentive, try some clapping rhymes. Introduce this next rhyme by saying you're going to show the group how they can clap their hands, wiggle their fingers, and then make their hands disappear, as they hide them behind their back. Do the rhyme slowly the first time, so parents will join in on the words and babies will join in on the clapping and wiggling the second time around.

Fee, Fi, Fo, Fum

Fee, fi, fo, fum,	*Clap four times.*
See my fingers,	*Wiggle fingers.*
See my thumbs,	*Wiggle thumbs.*
Fee, fi, fo, fum.	*Clap four times.*
Good-bye fingers,	*Hide one hand at a time*
Good-bye thumbs.	*behind back.*

You can speak this clapping song/rhyme instead of singing it, but the tune that Bob McGrath uses is easy to learn. Acknowledge to parents that the manipulation of fingers will be hard for babies to do, so it's best in this baby program to point to each finger since babies can't touch thumbs, then pointers, and so on, one by one.

Come a Look a See

Come a look a see,
Here's my mama.
Come a look a see,
Here's my papa.
Come a look a see,
Brother tall.
Sister, baby,
I love them all.
(*The Baby Record*)

You can kiss the tips of your fingers at the end or fold your fingers together and say, "And they all come together for a great big hug."

Start your round of Mother Goose rhymes with a familiar rhyme that you can sing or say. Clap hands as you say or sing it or follow motions indicated here.

Baa Baa Black Sheep

Baa baa black sheep,
Have you any wool?
Yes sir, yes sir,   *Nod head yes.*
Three bags full.   *Hold up three fingers.*

One for my master   *Hold up fingers one at a time*
And one for my dame.   *to count to three.*
And one for the little boy
Who lives down the lane.   *Point with your finger.*

(*Repeat first verse.*)
(*The Baby Record*)

Although this next rhyme has almost no motions for baby and grownup to do, it's a familiar song that tells a compelling little story. Encourage your group to join in with you. As with so many others, this rhyme can be sung or said and a recording containing this song is listed below the words.

Little Boy Blue

Little boy blue, come blow your horn.
The sheep's in the meadow.
The cow's in the corn.
But where is the boy who looks after the sheep?
He's under the haystack, fast asleep.
(*Raffi's Singable Songs Collection*)

Keep everyone going with another traditional Mother Goose rhyme that you can sing or say about this familiar fellow who keeps falling off the wall. A recording is listed below the rhyme.

Humpty Dumpty

Humpty Dumpty sat on a wall.
Humpty Dumpty had a great fall.   *Roll hands as rolling down a hill.*
All the King's horses   *Wiggle fingers on one hand.*
And all the King's men   *Wiggle fingers on the other hand.*
Couldn't put Humpty together again.   *Fold hands together.*
(*Hap Palmer*)

This is just a silly little rhyme that should be said quickly. Introduce it that way. It's a bit tricky, so be sure to practice this so you don't find your tongue tripping over all these similar sounding syllables.

Higglety Pigglety Pop

Higglety pigglety pop.   *Clap hands in rhythm to words.*
The dog has eaten the mop.
The pig's in a hurry
The cat's in a flurry
Higglety pigglety pop!

Add another familiar Mother Goose rhyme here. Invite your babies and parents to roll their hands as they raise their arms and then lower them, as they tell the story of Jack and Jill who go up the hill and back down. This is another rhyme that you can sing or say. The recording listed here has a second verse that you can certainly use if you want, but with babies this age, the shorter the better. But this recording will be very helpful in learning the melody.

Jack and Jill

Jack and Jill went up the hill,
To fetch a pail of water.
Jack fell down and broke his crown,
And Jill came tumbling after.
(*Nursery Rhyme Time*)

After this sustained period of sitting and doing clapping and Mother Goose rhymes, it's time to get the group up and moving around. So invite everyone in the circle to stand up and join hands, so they can do some circle games. There will be some children who won't want to join in. Make sure to assure their caregivers and parents that it's okay if they are hesitant to participate. Many babies at age eighteen months to two years have never or rarely been part of a circle activity like this and they will be shy about joining. It's a good idea, then, for them to watch the first time the group does the following song. Perhaps they will join in the second time around. Other babies will panic when everyone gets up and insist on being carried. Encourage their parents to do that. Everyone's comfort is your goal here; it's not 100 percent participation. Also, please note that the recording listed will give you the words and music to *The Muffin Man*, with the original words, not these words. But if you're hesitant about the melody, listening to it will make the melody fresher in your mind.

The Big Ship
(melody: The Muffin Man)

The big ship sails on the alley, alley oh   *Parents and children join hands*
The alley, alley oh,   *and walk around the circle.*
The alley, alley oh,
The big ship sails on the alley, alley oh
On the last day of September.
(*Ella Jenkins' Nursery Rhymes*)

After the opening circle time song, everyone stands in place for this next rhyme. As an introduction to the more active rhymes, the familiar tune of *The Farmer in the Dell* will help everyone to sing along. It works just as well if you chant it.

I Put My Arms up High
(melody: The Farmer in the Dell)

I put my arms up high.   *Raise arms up.*
I put my arms down low.   *Lower arms.*
I put my arms out to the side.   *Stick arms out to side.*
And then I let them go.   *Drop arms down.*
(*Early Early Childhood Songs*)

This next rhyme is great fun, as you and the other grownups reach up to the sky, inviting the babies to imitate you. When you stretch up high, make your voice go up high. When you reach down low, make your voice go low too. The grownups will do the same. The first time you do this rhyme, do it slowly and encourage the little ones to imitate you. Once they get the idea, they'll be more willing to join in the second time around.

Bend and Stretch

Bend and stretch, way up high.   *Reach hands as high as you can,*
Stand on tiptoe, touch the sky.   *stretching up on tiptoe.*

Bend and stretch, way down low.   *Bring hands down to feet and,*
Reach way down and touch your toes.   *crouching down, touch toes.*

Do this next rhyme as a call and response by inviting parents to repeat each line after you say it, as they imitate you in the simple actions in this rhyme. To help you get the rhythm, the "call" line is followed by the "response" line in parentheses. Do this rhyme extra slowly the first time, so everyone can get the idea of it. Babies love to imitate, though, so everyone will enjoy it.

I Clap My Hands

I clap my hands, (I clap my hands,)   *Clap hands.*
I touch my feet, (I touch my feet,)   *Touch feet.*
I jump up from the ground.
(I jump up from the ground.)   *Jump up.*
I clap my hands, (I clap my hands,)   *Clap hands.*
I touch my feet, (I touch my feet,)   *Touch feet.*
And turn my self around.
(And turn my self around.)   *Turn in place.*

This is plenty of activity for everyone, so invite everyone to join hands and go back to their places with another circle song. You can repeat the one you've already done, or do something that's more familiar like this song.

Here We Go Round the Mulberry Bush

Here we go round the mulberry bush,
The mulberry bush, the mulberry bush.
Here we go round the mulberry bush,
So early in the morning.
(Ella Jenkins' Nursery Rhymes)

Repeat this song at least twice and once the song is over, invite the group to sit back down. It's time for stories. But it's also time for puppets. The introduction of puppets into a baby program can be risky but the rewards are high. The babies will be fascinated with them, especially if they are small, so be prepared for many, if not all, of the babies to come up to you once the puppet has "come out" to say hello. There are a variety of finger puppets that you can use, from monkey mitts to small puppets that go on individual fingers, to small puppets that are puppies in a basket or mice in a box. It's best to hide these away from the group in a small bag before they make their appearance into the program and after they are done the children should say good-bye to them so they can "go to sleep" back in the bag while the rest of the program continues. All of the puppets mentioned in these programs are Folkmanis puppets and the information about this company is listed in the appendix on page 139. Here, the puppet is Three Puppies in a Basket. Make sure that every child who wants to has a chance to pet or touch the puppet. It takes some tactful crowd control at first, but babies soon learn they'll get a chance if they're patient enough.

After everyone has touched or petted or hugged the puppet, encourage everyone to sit down. It's nice to sing a song or do a rhyme about the puppet. There are many rhymes and songs that go perfectly with puppets. For this one, I've changed a well-known song just slightly to fit the occasion. Again, the recording listed will give you the melody for *A Tisket, a Tasket* with the original words.

Three Puppies Song

A tisket, a tasket,
Three puppies in a basket.
They wave their heads to say hello,
From in their cozy basket.
(*Here is Thumbkin*)

As soon as everyone has had a chance to pet the puppies and you've sung the song a couple of times, it's time for the puppies to be put away and the group is ready for a few stories. Although you can read slightly longer stories to walkers than prewalkers, the books recommended for these programs will still be fairly simple, with large, bright illustrations, and a simple text that babies can understand. Here are two that fit the bill. More are listed in the bibliography in the appendix.

Busy Lizzie, by Holly Berry. New York: North-South Books, 1994. As busy Lizzie goes through her day, she claps her hands and kicks her feet, activities listeners can do along with busy Lizzie, until she goes to sleep in her nice warm bed.

The Itsy Bitsy Spider, by Lorianne Siomades. Honesdale, PA: Boyds Mill Press, 1999. A perfect, baby-friendly rendition of the well-known rhyme with one line of the rhyme on each double page spread and bright collage illustrations that accompany them.

After you read the books aloud to the group, you can hand out books to the group as you did with the prewalkers, to reinforce the reading activity and give the children a chance to hold their own book in their hands. After this activity, invite everyone to stand back up for a final circle time activity. Here it's *Ring around the Rosie,* sure to be a hands down favorite with every group.

Ring around the Rosie

Ring around the rosie   *Grownups and children hold hands*
A pocket full of posies   *and go around the circle.*
Ashes, ashes,
We all fall down.   *Everyone falls down.*
(*Baby Face*)

After two rousing renditions of this favorite, invite everyone who has not "fallen down" to sit down. To end your program, do a final rhyme and your *Good-Bye Song*. Be sure, before you do these final rhymes and your *Good-Bye Rhyme,* to thank everyone for joining your program, invite them to borrow books, and make any announcements that are necessary, such as the date and time of the next program or registration dates that are upcoming.

Open, Shut Them

Open, shut them; open, shut them.   *Open and close fists.*
Give a little clap, clap, clap.   *Clap hands.*
Open, shut them; open, shut them.   *Open and close fists.*
Put them in your lap, lap, lap.   *Put hands in lap.*

Creep them, crawl them,   *Creep fingers up chest.*
Creep them, crawl them,
Right up to your chin, chin, chin,   *Tap chin with fingers.*
Open up your little mouth,
But do not let them in.   *Hide hands behind back.*
(Circle Time)

Good-Bye Song
(melody: London Bridge)

Good-bye, Good-bye,   *Lots of waving and blowing kisses.*
We'll see you soon,
See you soon, see you soon.
Good-bye, Good-bye,
We'll see you soon,
On another day!
(Toddler Tunes)

WALKER PROGRAM #2

Hello Song
(melody: London Bridge)

Hi, hello and how are you?   *Adults and babies wave hello.*
How are you? How are you?
Hi, hello and how are you?
How are you today?
(Toddler Tunes)

This is another great song to use as your introductory or "warmup" song, since so many children, tots, and parents know it. There are literally dozens of verses to this popular and well-known song. Sing about three or four of them, before the group becomes bored with it. Always end with a repetition of the first verse, to bring them back to the familiar. It is available on many recordings and one of them is listed underneath the song.

The Wheels on the Bus

The wheels on the bus   *Parents and babies roll hands.*
Go round and round,
Round and round,
Round and round.
The wheels on the bus
Go round and round,
All over town.   *Trace a circle with both arms.*

Other suggested verses:
The babies on the bus go
Waa, waa, waa.

The kids on the bus go
Yakety, yak, yak.

The grownups on the bus
Say, "I love you."

The horn on the bus goes
Beep, beep, beep.
(*Toddler Tunes*)

After such a familiar and popular opening song, your group should be happy, relaxed, warmed up, and attentive. Follow with some clapping rhymes like these next two rhymes. The first of these two won't be as familiar, so you should demonstrate it to everyone the first time you do it. Babies don't know their right hand from their left, but their grownups will, so remind grownups to help baby with this rhyme after they've watched you do it.

Right Hand, Left Hand

Right hand, left hand,	*Put each hand out, palms up.*
Put them on your head.	*Place hands on head.*
Right hand, left hand,	*Put each hand out, palms up.*
Put them all to bed.	*Put hands under head as if sleeping.*
Right hand, left hand,	*Put each hand out, palms up.*
Put them on your chest.	*Place hands on chest.*
Right hand, left hand,	*Put each hand out, palms up.*
Put them all to rest.	

This familiar rhyme is a great follow-up to a rhyme that's new and a perfect rhyme to do, since it will match well with all the other food rhymes and songs coming up.

Pat-a-Cake

Pat-a-cake, pat-a-cake.	*Clap in rhythm to the words.*
Baker's man.	
Bake me a cake	
As fast as you can.	
Roll it and pat it,	*Roll and gently pat hands together.*
And mark it with a B.	*Trace B on palm.*
And put it in the oven	*Extend both hands as if reaching out.*
For Baby and me.	*Point to baby and self.*

Introduce this rhyme as a good one to use in cold weather, when we need to warm ourselves up with a little porridge. Start the rhythm of the clapping to get everyone joined in, even before you start the rhyme. Remind parents they can use this rhyme at home, especially when cooking or serving food with their toddler.

Pease Porridge Hot

Pease porridge hot,	*Clap hands in rhythm to the words.*
Pease porridge cold.	
Pease porridge in the pot,	
Nine days old.	

Some like it hot.
Some like it cold.
Some like it in the pot,
Nine days old!

Continue the food idea with these two familiar traditional songs. The first can be sung and there's a recording listed that contains this song. The second is a spoken rhyme. Both are full of pretending and fun. Remind parents that all these "food" rhymes are great to use around the house. Baby may not really *like* tea but these next two rhymes are great opportunities for pretend, something he will like.

Polly Put the Kettle On

Polly put the kettle on.	*Make motions to imitate setting things*
Polly put the kettle on.	*on a table.*
Polly put the kettle on.	
We'll all have tea.	
Sukey take it off again.	*Make motions to imitate clearing*
Sukey take it off again.	*things away.*
Sukey take it off again.	
They've all gone away.	
Let's all wave goodbye.	*Wave goodbye.*
(*Toddler Tunes*)	

As is true with so many traditional rhymes, this next rhyme has a couple of different versions. This simplified version is easiest for baby to play along with and it tells a nice little story that has a fun slant on sharing and giving that baby is beginning to understand.

Here's a Cup

Here's a cup	*Make a circle with each hand for cups.*
And here's a cup	*Then hold them in front of you.*
I've got two cups of tea.	
Drink one cup.	*Pretend to hand to baby.*
Drink another cup.	*Pretend to hand to baby.*
Now I'll get one for me!	*Point at self.*

There's nothing that babies and toddlers like better than playing in water, so this next rhyme is a great choice for parents to bring home, as well as a good ending for all the "food" rhymes used here. If the parents wash dishes in the sink, babies always want to help, so tell them not to forget to sing this song. Have fun with the pretending idea of this rhyme, saying the word "ding" with a real ringing sound, as well as blowing kisses to the group after the line, "Three good kisses." A singing version of this rhyme is in the recording, *Nursery Rhyme Time*, called "Three Good Wishes," which uses a call-and-response technique and suggestions for motions to use.

Wash the Dishes

Wash the dishes,	*Rub hands together in circular motion.*
Wipe the dishes,	
Ring the bell for tea, ding!	*Pretend to pull string on bell.*
Three good wishes.	*Hold up three fingers.*
Three good kisses.	*Blow kisses.*
I will give to thee!	*Point to self on "I" and baby on "thee."*
(Nursery Rhyme Time)	

After all that listening and pretending, it's time to get everybody up and marching around. Use this song, sung to the tune of *If You're Happy and You Know it*. Ask all the grownups and kids to stand up and, with each child holding their grownup's hand, start around in a circle.

Marching Song
(melody: If You're Happy and You Know it)

Let's all march down the street,	*Grownups and children hold hands*
Down the street.	*and go around in a circle.*
Let's all march down the street,	
Down the street.	
Let's all march down the street,	
Wave at everyone we meet,	*Wave hands.*
Let's all march down the street.	
Down the street.	
(Get a Good Start)	

Ask everyone to remain standing for the next two songs. The first is an up and down song that is a great favorite with walkers. Many times, they will raise their arms up and forget to go down to the floor or vice versa, but with a little practice, they soon get the hang of this. You may want to do this rhyme more than twice, since everyone will have so much fun with it. If you want to sing it, use the tune, *Here We Go Looby-Loo* and a suggested recording of that is noted.

Up, Up, Up

Here we go up, up, up,	*With everyone standing, raise arms up.*
Here we go down, down, down.	*Lower arms and reach down to touch*
Here we go up, up, up,	*floor.*
Here we go down, down, down.	*With everyone standing, raise arms up.*
(*Get a Good Start*)	*Lower arms and reach down to touch*
	floor.

The next uses the familiar tune of *The Wheels on the Bus* but with different words. It can also be spoken and used as more of a call and response with parents repeating the "clap, clap, clap" or "stamp, stamp, stamp" phrases after you as they lead the children in those actions.

They're a Part of Me
(melody: Wheels on the Bus)

I can make my hands	
Go clap, clap, clap.	*Clap hands on "clap."*
Clap, clap, clap.	
Clap, clap, clap.	
I can make my hands	
Go clap, clap, clap.	
They're a part of me.	
I can make my feet	*Do actions for other verses*
Go stamp, stamp, stamp.	*as appropriate.*
I can make my legs	
Go hop, hop, hop.	
(*Toddler Tunes*)	

Before you end these action rhymes, do this childhood favorite, a perfect match to all those food and drink rhymes and songs you've done in this program. This is hard for little ones to do, with muscle movements that are a bit complicated, so don't be surprised if your walkers cannot put one hand on their hip and the other hand out like a spout!

I'm a Little Teapot

I'm a little teapot
Short and stout.
Here is my handle.   *One hand on hip*
Here is my spout.   *The other arm out to side.*

When I get all steamed up,
Hear me shout.
"Just tip me over
And pour me out."
(*Toddler Tunes*)

Use the same *Marching Song* or another song like *Here We Go Round the Mulberry Bush* to get everyone back to their places. If you like to use finger puppets, this is the time to introduce one. There are many really good puppets made by Folkmanis, like their Birds in a Nest puppet that is available with a few different colored birds. If you have that or a similar puppet, you might want to use this rhyme.

Birds in a Nest

Three little birds in a warm snug nest.
They stretch their wings
Then go back for a rest.
They stay right here and never fly.
Just wave their wings
And say "Goodbye."

When you introduce a puppet it's not really important whether or not you introduce a rhyme, but to give the children an opportunity to experience it. You may feel silly just holding up a puppet without a rhyme or song to go with it, but the toddlers will focus so completely on the puppet that they won't notice. Let them come up and touch it, if they wish. Be careful to let everyone have a chance. Make sure you say this to the group before you bring the puppet out, so the grownups will hear that and help to remind their child to share. Let the puppet have a limited time alone in the program and then do the rhyme or song, if you have one and urge everyone to say goodbye and the puppet goes back into the bag in which you carried it.

After the puppet, read a couple of books to the group. Try to get everyone to sit down, either on their grownups' laps or on the floor, but don't expect complete success on this one. When you have your group reasonably settled, here are two great books to share.

Barnyard Banter, by Denise Fleming. New York: Henry Holt, 1994. Fleming's bright, collage illustrations and interactive text combine to get lots of young listeners mooing, clucking, and quacking along with all the residents of the barnyard.

I Love Animals, by Flora McDonnell. Cambridge, MA: Candlewick Press, 1994. Each page introduces another familiar animal and shows why they are so loveable. This book's slightly enlarged format, clear illustrations, and readable text make this a perfect read aloud choice.

As always, if you wish to hand out books for everyone to share with their little ones together, please do that now. Babies love to be read to and grownups will feel more confident once they've watched you do it successfully. After the reading time, everyone's settled down and calm, so try some gentle, quiet rhymes before it's time to say good-bye.

The first pretend rhyme involves a lot of small motor movement, but little ones will love to watch their grownups do it and try to copy them.

Ten Little Gentlemen

Ten little gentlemen,	*Hold up ten fingers.*
Standing in a row.	
Bow little gentlemen,	*Bend fingers down.*
Bow down low.	
Walk little gentlemen,	*"Walk" fingers across floor.*
Right across the floor.	
But don't forget gentlemen,	
Please close the door.	*Clap hands once.*

(The second time you do this rhyme, make it, "Ten Little Ladies.")

After all the "food" stuff that's been going on in this program, this is a good choice for one of your closing rhymes. If you have a little spider finger puppet, here's a perfect chance to use it!

Little Miss Muffet

Little Miss Muffet
Sat on her tuffet,
Eating her curds and whey.
Along came a spider,
And sat down beside her.
And frightened Miss Muffet away.

Right before you say good-bye, settle everyone down with this little song, using a familiar tune.

I Wiggle My Fingers
(melody: Here We Go Round the Mulberry Bush)

I wiggle my fingers,	*Wiggle fingers.*
I wiggle my toes,	*Point to toes.*
I wiggle my shoulders,	*Shrug shoulders.*
I wiggle my nose.	*Wiggle nose.*
Now no more wiggles	*Shake head "no."*
Are left in me.	
So I'll be as still	*Fold hands together*
As still as can be.	*in lap.*
(*Toddler Tunes*)	

Use this time to make any announcements you might have, including the date of the next program, or other programs your patrons may be interested in. Remind them to borrow books before they leave. Always use the same good-bye song.

Good-Bye Song
(melody: London Bridge)

Good-bye, Good-bye,	*Lots of waving and blowing kisses.*
We'll see you soon,	
See you soon, see you soon.	
Good-bye, Good-bye,	
We'll see you soon,	
On another day!	
(*Toddler Tunes*)	

WALKER PROGRAM #3

Hello Song
(melody: London Bridge)

Hi, hello and how are you?   *Adults and babies wave hello.*
How are you? How are you?
Hi, hello and how are you?
How are you today?
(*Toddler Tunes*)

   This warmup song is another well-known childhood favorite. It can be found in many recordings and one of them is listed underneath the words to the song.

If You're Happy and You Know It

If you're happy and you know it,
Clap your hands.   *Clap, clap.*
If you're happy and you know it,
Clap your hands.   *Clap, clap.*
If you're happy and you know it
And you really want to show it,
If you're happy and you know it,
Clap your hands.   *Clap, clap.*

Do a few more verses, like:

Tap your feet.
Blow a kiss.
Shout hoorah.
(*If You're Happy*)

   As in the other programs, after this warmup song, a few clapping rhymes are in order. Encourage parents to clap along with their babies, or in some cases, for those babies who may not be clapping as well as the others in the group. Introduce the first rhyme as a clapping and counting rhyme. Help the group to focus by inviting little ones to sit down and show off their shoes.

One, Two, Buckle My Shoe

One, two, buckle my shoe.   *Tap shoes.*
Three, four, shut the door.   *Clap hands twice.*
Five, six, pick up sticks.   *Put hands out, palms down, and*
Seven, eight, lay them straight.   *wiggle fingers.*
Nine, ten, a big fat hen.   *Lay palms flat on floor.*
                                             Brings hands wider apart on the last
                                             three words.

Where Is Thumbkin?

Where is thumbkin?   *Bring out one thumb, then the other.*
Where is thumbkin?
Here I am.   *"Nod" one thumb to the other.*
Here I am.
How are you today, sir?
Very well, I thank you.
Go away.   *Hide one hand, then the other*
Go away.   *behind back.*

(Repeat with other fingers if desired.)
(Where is Thumbkin)

These pretend rhymes combine some traditional Mother Goose rhymes with some other rhymes about the outdoors, making them great for parents to use when they take their little ones outside. But before we go out, we should look our best. Since brushing hair is not always a little one's favorite thing to do, introduce this rhyme as a way to make it easier.

Brush Hair, Brush

Brush hair, brush.   *Pretend to brush hair.*
It's time for us to go.
If you want to look your best,
Brush your hair so.

Especially in spring and summer, there will be plenty of flowers for babies and toddlers to investigate, whether they're in pots, garden plots or growing wild in a park. Here's an easy rhyme for parent/caregiver and baby to do together as they inspect all of nature's finery.

Green Leaf

Here's a leaf,	*Hold one palm out flat.*
And here's a leaf,	*Hold another palm out flat.*
And that makes two.	*Bring flat hands together, palms up.*
Here's a bud.	*Bring palms together.*
It makes a flower.	*Open hands, keep wrists together.*
Watch it bloom for you.	*Raise hands slightly upward.*

On your imaginary walk outside during your program or when caregiver and child go walking together, the rhyme or song about Mary and her little lamb is always a fun song to share. Only the first verse is shown here, although there are two more. One is probably enough for little ones.

Mary Had a Little Lamb

Mary had a little lamb,
Its fleece was white as snow.
And everywhere that Mary went,
The lamb was sure to go.
(Hap Palmer Sings Classic Nursery Rhymes)

Another thing that's sure to be seen outside in spring or summer are the bees. Although this next rhyme can be done as a flannel board rhyme for older children, it's not really appropriate for little ones under two and a half. Here, the pretend rhyme complete with motions is enough with plenty of buzzing at the end.

Here Is the Beehive

Here is the beehive,	*Hold up closed fist.*
But where are the bees?	
They're hiding inside,	*Point to fist.*
Where nobody sees.	
Watch them come out of the hive.	
1-2-3-4-5.	*Slowly unfold fingers.*
Bzzzzzzz!	*"Fly" fingers around.*

It's time to get everyone up and moving around now. Ask everyone to stand up and join hands for this circle song.

Down by the Station

Down by the station,
Early in the morning,
See the little puffer-bellies,
All in a row.
See the station master,
Pull the little handle,
Chug, chug, toot, toot.
Here we go.
(Here is Thumbkin)

While everyone is standing up, invite them to join in these whole-body rhymes. This first rhyme should be done slowly and make sure to remind the grownups that they should help children if they're not sure where their head, shoulders, knees, and toes are or if they get stuck on head and don't move on!

Head, Shoulders, Knees, and Toes

Head, shoulders, knees, and toes,   *Touch parts of body as indicated.*
Knees and toes.
Head, shoulders, knees, and toes,
Knees and toes.
Here's my eyes, my ears,
My mouth, and my nose.
Head, shoulders, knees, and toes,
Knees and toes.
(Where is Thumbkin)

This familiar nursery song becomes a whole-body experience. Invite parents to hold their children's hands so they are facing one another and as parent and child join hands and rock from one foot to the other, they can chant, "tick/tock" a couple of time before they sing this song.

Hickory Dickory Dock

Tick-tock, tick-tock.   *Adult and child hold hands and face*
Tick-tock, tick-tock.   *one another.*
                                         Rock from one foot to the other.
Hickory, dickory, dock.   *Continue rocking throughout the song.*
The mouse ran up the clock.
The clock struck one.
The mouse ran down.
Hickory, dickory, dock.
(Playtime Activity Rhymes)

Before returning everyone to their places, see how many children will jump along with you in this rhyme. It takes a lot of energy, but it's a lot of fun to watch little ones jump while you say this rhyme.

Jump, Jump

Jump, jump, Kangaroo Brown.
Jump, jump, up and down.
Jump, jump, Kangaroo Brown.
Jump, jump all around.

You can bring everyone back to their places using *Down by the Station* or another song. But after all that jumping, you can just have everyone sit right where they are.

If you have introduced puppets in other programs, your little ones will be eager to see another puppet. If you have a small bunny finger puppet, you can try the first rhyme shown here. But if you have the bunny in hat puppet, you can try the second rhyme.

Bunny Rhyme

Here is a bunny with ears so funny
And here is his hole in the ground.
When a noise he hears,
He pricks up his ears,
And jumps in his hole in the ground.

Bunny in Hat

Here is a bunny
With ears so funny
And here is his magic hat,
When a noise he hears,
He pricks up his ears,
And disappears—
Just like that!

After your puppet has had his moment in the spotlight, hide him back in the bag in which you brought him and bring out a story. Here are two that will work well.

In the Tall, Tall Grass, by Denise Fleming. New York: Henry Holt & Co., 1991. Another inviting, interactive book, with lots of actions by the animals in the book, lots of sound words, and beautiful collage illustrations with Fleming's handmade paper.

Time For Bed, by Mem Fox. Illustrated by Jane Dyer. San Diego: Harcourt Brace Jovanovich, 1993. Although available in big book and board book, use the standard format as you read this aloud, with a couple of board book copies to hand out afterward so babies and parents can share it together. A beautiful book in which all the animals say goodnight secure in the love of their parents.

Use the quiet of this time to hand everyone their own board book to share with their baby. When that reading time is done, do some quiet finger plays.

Wiggle, Wiggle Fingers

Wiggle, wiggle fingers, *Wiggle fingers up in the air.*
Right up to the sky,
Way up high.
Wiggle, wiggle fingers,
Wave them all good-bye. *Wave goodbye.*
Wiggle, wiggle fingers, *Wiggle fingers.*
Right into a ball. *Fold fingers into a ball.*
Now throw them in your lap. *Place folded hands in lap.*
But do not let them fall. *Shake head no.*

Invite everyone to "get their spiders out" and demonstrate different ways you can make a spider crawling up the spout. If you have a spider finger puppet and want to use it, go ahead.

The Itsy-Bitsy Spider

The itsy-bitsy spider	*Crawl spider up.*
Went up the water spout.	
Down came the rain	*Wiggle fingers down for rain.*
And washed the spider out.	
Out came the sun,	*Hands up in a big circle.*
And dried up all the rain,	
And the itsy-bitsy spider	
Went up the spout again.	*Crawl spider up.*
(Best Toddler Tunes)	

Before you sing your goodbye song, make any announcements you need to make about upcoming programs and registration dates and as always, encourage your patrons to borrow books.

Good-Bye Song
(melody: London Bridge)

Good-bye, Good-bye,	*Lots of waving and blowing kisses.*
We'll see you soon,	
See you soon, see you soon.	
Good-bye, Good-bye,	
We'll see you soon,	
On another day!	

WALKER PROGRAM #4

Hello Song
(melody: London Bridge)

Hi, hello and how are you?	*Adults and babies wave hello.*
How are you? How are you?	
Hi, hello and how are you?	
How are you today?	
(Toddler Tunes)	

This welcoming song can be sung to the tune of *Here We Go Round the Mulberry Bush*. It warms up singing voices, clapping hands, and tapping feet. As with all the other warmup songs suggested in other programs, it's flexible enough to use as few or as many verses as you want to do and will give your group a chance to feel comfortable.

Sing with Me
(melody: Here We Go Round the Mulberry Bush)

Come along and sing with me,
Sing with me, sing with me.
Come along and sing with me,
This bright and sunny morning.

Come along and clap with me . . .   *Do actions as indicated.*

Come along and tap your feet . . .

Come along and stretch up high . . .
(Ella Jenkins' Nursery Rhymes)

Babies and toddlers are fascinated not only with the animals and plants that grow outside but the different weather days they encounter on their walks, rides, and playtimes in the park or the neighborhood playground. The pretend rhymes included here explore some of the weather they'll find. Before we go outside and explore the weather, let's continue the warmup with these two rhymes. First, let's make sure our fingers and hands are warmed up with this finger play.

I Have Ten Fingers

I have ten fingers,
And they all belong to me.   *Hold up ten fingers.*
I can make them do things.   *Wiggle fingers.*
So do this now with me.
First, raise them up high,   *Raise hands up high.*
Then bring them down low,   *Lower hands.*
Then make them all hide,   *Put hands behind back.*
And fold them just so.   *Fold hands in lap.*

Invite everyone to stand up and put their hands on their shoulders. In rhythm to the words, invite everyone to stretch their arms up in the air and bring them back down. Many toddlers get so carried away with this rhyme, they start bending their knees up and down, too.

Exercises, Exercises

Exercises, exercises,
Let's all do our exercises.
Exercises, exercises,
Let's all do our exercises.

After everyone has sat back down, invite everyone to take an imaginary walk outside and see the raindrops and sunshine. This first song combines them both. This is a great song to use on walks outside or even at home in the bathtub, where plenty of splashing is in order.

Rain/Shine Song

Rain is falling down—splash.	*Lower both hands with wiggling fingers.*
Rain is falling down—splash.	*Slap floor or lap on "splash."*
Pitter patter, pitter patter.	*Clap hands.*
Rain is falling down—splash.	*Lower both hands with wiggling fingers.*
Sun is peeking out—peek.	*Cover eyes with hands and*
Sun is peeking out—peek.	*remove them on "peek."*
Peeking here and peeking there.	*Cover eyes and remove hands on*
	"here" and "there."
Sun is peeking out—peek.	*Cover eyes with hands and*
(The Baby Record)	*remove them on "peek."*

After the rain and sun, sometimes beautiful things grow. But before they grow big, they start out as seeds. This next pretend rhyme can be a simple finger play or a whole-body rhyme. Depending on the size and mood of your group, everyone may not want to crouch down and then rise up, and just using your hands may work better. This rhyme is shown here with both sets of directions.

Little Brown Seed

I'm a little brown seed,   *Crouch down.*
Rolled up in a tiny ball.
The rain and the sunshine   *Rise slowly to standing.*
Will make me big and tall.   *Reach arms over head.*

Here's a little brown seed,   *Hold up hand in a fist.*
Rolled up in a tiny ball.   *Cover fist with other hand.*
The rain and the sunshine   *Wiggle fingers for rain and make a*
Will make me big and tall.   *circle for sun.*
                                             Reach both hands over head.

The rain is an endless source of fascination for toddlers. It changes the way everything looks; it makes noise as it patters against the windows; it makes you wet. Such a wonderful phenomenon is a great reason for singing. Here are two more rain songs to help you celebrate the rain.

Pitter Patter
(melody: The Muffin Man)

Pitter patter falls the rain   *Flutter fingers down for rain.*
On the roof and window pane.
Softly, softly it comes down.
It makes the stream go round and   *Trace circle with finger.*
   round.
(Ella Jenkins Nursery Rhymes)

This next rhyme is a spoken one. Introduce this as a great rhyme to say as parent and toddler take a walk in the rain under their umbrella. Tell them to point to each thing in the rhyme as they say it. It's a wonderful vocabulary reinforcement used that way. Here, in the program, simply flutter your fingers like raindrops until the last line of the rhyme, as you point to yourself.

Rain on the Rooftops

Rain on the rooftops,   *Flutter hands down like rain while*
Rain on the tree.   *you say each line.*
Rain on the green grass,
But not on me.   *Point to self and shake head no.*

By this time in the program, everyone needs to move around a little. Invite caregivers to stand, hold hands with their children, and form a circle. Reluctant or shy children can sit out the first time or encourage the grownups to pick them up and carry them around the circle. This walking song can be sung to the tune of *Skip to My Lou* and is easy to learn so parents and children can sing it as they walk together outside.

Two by Two
(melody: Skip to My Lou)

Walking along, two by two.   *Walk around in the circle, with*
Walking along, two by two.   *grownup holding child's hand.*
Walking along, two by two.
Skip to my Lou, my darling.

Everyone's welcome, you come too.
Everyone's welcome, you come too.
Everyone's welcome, you come too.
Skip to my Lou, my darling.
(*Get a Good Start*)

What's a better song to sing in this program than *Mister Sun*? This is so universally known that many toddlers will come into your program having heard it on favorite recordings and television programs and may have sung it at home. The recording noted here is done by Raffi, who is best known for it, although many other recordings include it as well. While everyone's standing, invite them to make big circles over their heads and join in with this favorite.

Mister Sun

Oh, Mister Sun, Sun,	*Make a circle above your head with*
Mister Golden Sun,	*your arms.*
Please shine down on me.	*Flutter hands down like "sunbeams."*
Oh, Mister Sun, Sun,	*Make a circle above your head with*
Mister Golden Sun,	*your arms.*
Hiding behind a tree.	*Hide face behind hands.*
These little children are asking you,	*Point to children.*
To please come out so they can play	*Beckon with arm.*
with you.	
Oh, Mister Sun, Sun,	*Make a circle above your head with*
Mister Golden Sun,	*your arms.*
Please shine down on me.	*Flutter hands down like "sunbeams."*
(Singable Songs for the Very Young)	

This next rhyme is short but lots of fun as the babies and their parents celebrate all those great things they can do already, like clapping, stamping, and jumping. What could be better than that?

With Our Hands

With our hands, we clap, clap, clap.	*Clap three times.*
With our feet, we stamp, stamp, stamp.	*Stamp foot three times.*
We jump three times as high as can be.	*Jump three times.*
Then we say,	
"Hey, look at me."	*Point to self.*

You can invite everyone to sit down right where they are or repeat the *Two by Two* song to end this activity portion of the program. Once everyone is settled, it's time for a couple of books and, if you want to use one, a small finger puppet. If you have the Folkmanis puppet that is a pot filled with four flowers, this is a rhyme that should fit perfectly. Other flower puppets will work well, too. The rhyme can be sung to the tune of *London Bridge*, if you wish to sing it. But it's just as fun to recite it.

Four Flowers in a Pot
(melody: London Bridge)

Four little flowers
Smiling at me.
Waiting for the rain
As dry as can be.
Down, down, down,
Comes the gentle rain.
Four little flowers
Lift their heads again.

After you've given everyone a chance to touch the puppet and said or sung the rhyme, put the puppet back into your bag, so it disappears from view. Invite everyone to sit down, either on the floor or on a lap, for some stories.

Here Are My Hands, by Bill Martin and Ted Archambault. Illustrated by Ted Rand. New York: Henry Holt, 1987. This classic book uses a rhyming text to introduce hands, feet, knees, and other important parts of baby's body. The text invites interaction with the child and the multiracial cast used in the illustrations is equally appealing.

Piggies, by Don and Audrey Wood. New York: San Diego: Harcourt Brace Jovanovich, 1991. A humorous take on the classic piggies nursery rhyme that babies and parents can join in with as you read.

Some groups may need more book interaction, so take this time to give each of your parents and caregivers a book to share with their child. This is a quiet, informal time when babies will be receptive to sharing a book with their grownups and will probably find time to do a little socializing as well.

To signal an end to the reading time, remind parents and caregivers to take home some of the books they've shared with their babies today. Ask them to close the books they have with them now, so you can all do some closing rhymes. Some quiet finger plays or clapping rhymes are best, such as the two suggested here. For the first rhyme, invite everyone to hold up their hands, closed up tight into fists. This is also a familiar rhyme to many parents, but make sure to do it twice, as with all finger plays.

Do this one at normal speed the first time through. The second time, start out quickly and at "creep them, crawl them" say the lines slowly until the last line, "Do not let them in," which is said really quickly as you hide them behind your back.

Open, Shut Them

Open, shut them,	*Open and close fists.*
Open, shut them,	
Give a little clap, clap, clap.	*Clap hands.*
Open, shut them,	*Open and close fists.*
Open, shut them,	
Put them in your lap, lap, lap.	*Interlace fingers and put hands in lap.*
Creep them, crawl them.	*Walk fingers up chest.*
Creep them, crawl them.	
Right up to your chin, chin, chin.	*Touch fingers to chin.*
Open up your little mouth.	*Open mouth.*
But do not let them in!	*Hide hands behind back.*

This Little Pig

This little pig went to market,	*Touch baby's fingers, one by one.*
This little pig stayed home.	
This little pig had roast beef.	
This little pig had none.	
And this little pig cried,	
"Wee, wee, wee,"	*Run fingers up baby's arm and tickle*
All the way home.	*under chin.*

Before singing your good-bye song, thank parents and caregivers for coming to the program and remind them of future program dates or registration dates. If they've had a chance to look at board books during your program, invite them to bring them home. If not, remind them to share books with their babies after the program and, of course, to bring some books home.

Good-Bye Song
(melody: London Bridge)

Good-bye, good-bye,   *Lots of waving and blowing kisses.*
We'll see you soon,
See you soon, see you soon.
Good-bye, good-bye,
We'll see you soon,
On another day!
(*Toddler Tunes*)

PROGRAM #5

Hello Song
(melody: London Bridge)

Hi, hello,   *Wave hand in rhythm of song.*
And how are you?
How are you? How are you?
Hi, hello,
And how are you?
How are you today?
(*Toddler Tunes*)

Two warmup songs are shown here. This first song is sung to *Row, Row, Row Your Boat* and you can use as many verses as you and your group want to include. If you sing both this and the following warmup song, you might want to sing only one or two verses.

Roll, Roll, Roll Your Hands
(melody: Row, Row, Row your Boat)

Roll, roll, roll your hands
As fast as fast can be.
Do it now, let me see.
Do it now with me.

Clap, clap, clap your hands
As loud as loud can be.
Do it now, let me see.
Do it now with me.

Tap, tap, tap your feet.
As softly as can be.
Do it now, let me see.
Do it now with me.
(Toddler Tunes)

This well-known song has many different versions, but the simplest version is shown here. Although this sometimes uses humor in the text, the repetition is more effective for this age group. Although you can use the "put your finger on your nose" version as well, this rendition uses clothing.

Put Your Finger on Your Shirt
(melody: If You're Happy and You Know It)

Put your finger on your shirt, on your shirt.
Put your finger on your shirt, on your shirt.
Put your finger on your shirt,
Put your finger on your shirt,
Put your finger on your shirt, on your shirt.

On your shoes . . .

On your pants . . .
(Children's All-Time Rhythm Favorites)

So many children's songs and rhymes celebrate the outdoors and some of them are included here. The wonderful element to these songs is their ability to travel home with baby and caregiver. From there, the songs and rhymes can go on walks, out to the playground, or for rides in the car. Two small finger plays begin the fun, and celebrate the birds and animals baby and parent are likely to see.

Five Little Robins

Five little robins	*Hold up five fingers.*
Lived in a tree.	
Father, Mother,	*Point to thumb, pinkie.*
And babies three.	*Hold up remaining three fingers.*
Father caught a worm,	*Hold up thumb.*
Mother caught a bug.	*Hold up pinkie.*
And the three little babies	*Hold up three fingers.*
Stayed home warm and snug.	*Curl fingers down into fist.*

Although it's doubtful that in the city or busy suburbs, a baby might encounter a rabbit on a regular basis, children's books are full of them. They're also a favorite in children's petting zoos and farms. This next rhyme is such a perfect little story, complete with dialogue, drama, and a surprise ending. It also makes a great puppet rhyme. This is sure to be a favorite in your program for years to come.

I Saw a Little Rabbit

I saw a little rabbit	*Make rabbit ears with two fingers.*
Go hop, hop, hop.	*Hop fingers along other arm.*
I saw his long ears	
Go flop, flop, flop.	*Bend fingers on "flop."*
I saw his little nose	
Go twink, twink, twink.	*Point to nose.*
I saw his little eyes go	
Wink, wink, wink.	*Point to eyes.*
I said, "Little Rabbit,	
Won't you stay?"	
But he looked at me,	
And hopped away!	*Hop fingers along arm.*

Another favorite element in children's books is a garden. So this garden verse is a handy one to use. It's great for parents to bring home and use as they plant anything, large or small, at home. Babies are fascinated by the idea of planting a seed in the ground and watching it grow, so this verse will soon become a favorite.

This Is My Garden

This is my garden,   *Hold hand out, palm up.*
I'll rake it with care.   *Rake fingers across palm.*
Then some flower seeds,   *Plant seeds on palm.*
I will plant there.
The sun will shine,   *Make circle above head with arms.*
And the rain will fall,   *Lower fingers for rain.*
And my flowers will grow   *Raise arms above head.*
Straight and tall.   *Wiggling fingers.*

Doing this next rhyme with everyone standing is a fun way to prepare for circle rhymes. As with so many of these rhymes, it combines a little story with a little pretending and a little movement. That winning combination makes it fun for everyone. Although your walkers may hesitate to crouch down at first, they will probably join in the second time you do this rhyme.

Flower Play

If I were a little flower,   *Crouch down close to the floor and*
Sleeping underneath the ground,   *bend head.*
I'd raise my head and grow and grow,   *Slowly raise up from floor.*
And stretch my arms and grow and   *Stand up and raise up arms.*
  grow,
And reach up to the sun.   *Raise up arms and raise face as if to*
                                       sky.

While everyone is standing, invite them to hold hands with their grownups for a pretend walk down the street. Of course, in the program, everyone will simply hold hands and walk around the circle.

Marching Song
(melody: If you're Happy and You Know it)

Let's all march down the street,	*Grownups and children hold hands*
Down the street.	*and walk around the circle.*
Let's all march down the street,	
Down the street.	
Let's all march down the street,	
Smile at everyone we meet.	
Let's all march down the street,	
Down the street.	

(*Children's All-Time Rhythm Favorites*)

Here are two standing rhymes that are the perfect follow-up to the *Marching Song*. For the first, ask everyone to stand up straight and tall. It's a simple little rhyme that is easy to follow and easy to remember and bring home.

I Put My Arms up High

I put my arms up high,	*Raise arms straight up.*
I put my arms down low.	*Drop arms straight down.*
I put them straight out to the side,	*Stick arms out to the side.*
And then I let them go.	*Drop arms loosely to sides.*

This standing rhyme has a little bit of pretend in it as it celebrates the outdoors and the pretty leaves that fall from the trees.

Little Leaves
(melody: London Bridge)

Little leaves fall gently down.	*Stand up, have hands flutter down.*
Gently down, gently down.	
Whirling, whirling, round and round,	*Turn around in place.*
Down, down, down.	*Stand up, have hands flutter down.*

This variation on a traditional nursery rhyme involves lots of rocking and lots of tick-tocking. Ask parents to hold their children's hands in their hands. The child can face them or face out to the circle. To begin this song, ask the parent-child pair to rock from foot to foot, and start them in a chant of "tick-tock, tick-tock."

Hickory Dickory Dock

Hickory dickory dock,   *Grownup and child hold hands.*
The mouse ran up the clock.   *The two rock from one foot to other*
The clock struck one,   *to rhythm of song while holding hands.*
The mouse ran down.
Hickory dickory dock.
(Best Toddler Tunes)

This rhyme is a classic and has appeared in books and recordings galore. There are several variations on it and the one included here is simple for you and your group to do. There's just a little bit of action but loads of fun.

Teddy Bear

Teddy bear, teddy bear,   *Do actions as indicated.*
Turn around.
Teddy bear, teddy bear,
Touch the ground.
Teddy bear, teddy bear,
Show me your shoe.
Teddy bear, teddy bear,
I love you.
Teddy bear, teddy bear,
Give a jump a try,
Teddy bear, teddy bear,
Wave good-bye.

Bring your group around the circle once again with the *Marching Song* or ask them to sit back down in their places without the song. It's time for puppets and books. There are so many Folkmanis puppets that are perfect for this age group. One of them is Three Bunnies in a Green Basket. You can put your three fingers inside the bunnies and manipulate them to bend and nod to your rhyme. Of course, if your group is already used to puppets, many of the babies will want to come up and pet or touch the puppets, so give them a chance to do that. Before bringing the puppet out, be sure to explain to parents that each child will get a chance with the puppet, so they don't need to crowd. Here's a rhyme to go with them.

Three Bunnies

Here's three bunnies in a basket green,
They're hopping up and down,
So happy to be seen.
If you wave your hand,
I'm sure they'll all say hi,
And when they're tired of hopping,
We will all say, "Good-bye."

Once the puppet is stored away, ask everyone to sit down for stories. Not everyone will sit. They're so excited about the book and so
anxious to see it and so unaccustomed to being read to in a group situation, they can't possibly settle down on their grownups' laps. Make
sure grownups know that it's okay for their little ones to walk closer to
you or stand in front of you, as long as they don't block anyone. You
can always kneel up to make yourself higher or even sit on a stool for
this portion of the program. Here are two wonderful books for this
age group.

I Love Trucks, by Philomon Sturges. Illustrated by Shari Halpern.
New York: HarperCollins, 1999. With its bright, childlike illustrations,
and simple declarative sentences that extol the great things about every
kind of truck, this book will be a hit for every vehicle lover, young and
old, in your group.

Brown Bear, Brown Bear, What Do You See? by Bill Martin. Illustrated by Eric Carle. New York: Holt Rinehart, Winston, 1983. This is a
classic picture book for this age group that is also a favorite with toddlers, preschoolers, and kindergarteners alike. It's been chanted, recited, and even sung by countless children and parents and your group
will love it.

Your group will be at its most attentive after two wonderful picture
books like these two. Take advantage of their attention and quiet to do
a couple of clapping rhymes or songs. Here are two that have been used
in previous programs. Sing this rhyme or chant it. Many children and
parents know it, but if they don't it's easy to use and a favorite from one
program to the next.

Open, Shut Them

Open, shut them,   *Open and close fists.*
Open, shut them,
Give a little clap, clap, clap.   *Clap hands.*
Open, shut them,   *Open and close fists.*
Open, shut them,
Put them in your lap, lap, lap.   *Interlace fingers and put hands in lap.*

Creep them, crawl them.   *Walk fingers up chest.*
Creep them, crawl them.
Right up to your chin, chin, chin.   *Touch fingers to chin.*
Open up your little mouth.   *Open mouth.*
But do not let them in!   *Hide hands behind back.*

This is another good rhyme for the end to any program. Encourage parents to wiggle their fingers and ask them to urge their babies to join them.

Wiggle, Wiggle Fingers

Wiggle, wiggle fingers,   *Wiggle fingers up in the air.*
Right up to the sky,
Way up high.
Wiggle, wiggle fingers,
Wave them all good-bye.   *Wave goodbye.*
Wiggle, wiggle fingers,   *Wiggle fingers.*
Right into a ball.   *Fold fingers into a ball.*
Now throw them in your lap.   *Place folded hands in lap.*
But do not let them fall.   *Shake head no.*

Be sure to thank the group for its attendance today. They are making a wonderful effort to show they care about their children and they want to surround them with language and books right from the beginning of their lives. Encourage parents and caregivers to borrow books, remind them of the date of future programs, and sing your good-bye song.

Good-Bye Song
(melody: London Bridge)

Good-bye, good-bye,   *Lots of waving and blowing kisses.*
We'll see you soon,
See you soon, see you soon.
Good-bye, good-bye,
We'll see you soon,
On another day!

4

RHYMES TO TAKE HOME

Although many, if not all, of the rhymes used in the programs in this book can be taken anywhere and used with babies, the rhymes spotlighted here are rhymes that parents and caregivers can easily attach to some household routine. Some rhymes and songs may be hard for parents not used to singing and chanting with their babies to use outside the context of the program. So the rhymes repeated here, culled from both prewalker and walker programs, are grouped by a particular time of day or activity.

As you do the programs, it's always a good idea to suggest to parents ways to use these rhymes at home—while bathing, changing, feeding, or carrying baby. Grouped as they are here, you can make handout sheets for parents and caregivers to bring home. It's true that many caregivers will have no problem carrying the rhymes and songs home with them. I think of the babysitter who explained to her young charge that they had to go shopping and led him out of the children's room, singing *To Market, To Market*. I'm reminded of the many parents who've said to me, "We sing that at home," after I've introduced a song. For those caregivers who find it a bit harder, maybe these divisions will make it clearer. The first section is for the tub and the changing table. From small rhymes for fingers and toes to a chant to help with brushing hair to songs for clothes, these will help parents make the getting dressed part of baby's day more fun and less of a trial. The second section will be food rhymes that will celebrate food that baby likes and some that she doesn't. The third section has rhymes to accompany parents and caregivers as they take their babies out and about, whether it's walking, or riding. The last section is for lullabies, to soothe baby to sleep after her busy day. A small selection of special occasion rhymes ends this section.

TAKE HOME RHYME LIST

**Tub and Changing
   Table Rhymes**
Brush Hair, Brush
Diddle Diddle Dumpling
One, Two Buckle my Shoe
Pitty Patty Polt
Put Your Finger on Your Shirt
Round About
Round and Round the Garden
Rub a Dub Dub
Rub a Dub Dub, Who's in
   the Tub?
Shoe the Old Horse
These Are Baby's Fingers
This Little Pig

Food Rhymes
Baté, Baté, Chocolaté
Here Is a Doughnut
Here's a Cup
Hot Cross Buns
I Eat My Peas with Honey
I'm a Little Teapot
Milkman, Milkman
Muffin Man
Pancake
Pease Porridge Hot

Polly Put the Kettle On
Wash the Dishes

Out and About Rhymes
Away up High
Away up High (Baby)
Here's a Leaf
I Hear Thunder
The Itsy-Bitsy Spider
Let's Take a Walk
Little Leaves
London Bridge
Marching Song
Mister Sun
The Rain
Rain on the Rooftops
Rain, Rain Go Away
Rain Is Falling Down
Red Says Stop
This Is My Garden
To Market, To Market

Lullabies
Hush-a-Bye
Lavender's Blue
Rock-a-Bye Baby
See Saw Margery Daw

Star Light
Twinkle, Twinkle Little Star

Special Occasion Rhymes
Five Little Pumpkins

Jack O'Lantern
Jack O'Lantern II
I Have a Little Heart
Valentines

TUB AND CHANGING TABLE RHYMES

Brush Hair, Brush

Brush hair, brush.
It's time for us to go.
If you want to look your best,
Brush your hair so.

Diddle Diddle Dumpling

Diddle diddle dumpling,
My son, John.
Went to bed with his trousers on.
One shoe off,
And one shoe on.
Diddle diddle dumpling,
My son, John.

Bicycle baby's legs.

Tap one foot.
Tap the other foot.
Bicycle baby's legs.

One, Two, Buckle My Shoe

One, two, buckle my shoe.
Three, four, shut the door.
Five, six, pick up sticks.
Seven, eight, lay them straight.
Nine, ten, a big fat hen.

Clap twice, tap shoes.
Clap twice, clap hands.
Clap hands, wiggle fingers.
Clap hands, pat hands on floor.
Clap hands, widen arms.

Pitty Patty Polt

Pitty patty polt,
Shoe the little colt,
Here a nail,
There a nail,
Pitty patty polt.

Tap baby's feet together.

Tap one foot.
Tap the other foot.
Tap baby's feet together.

Put Your Finger on Your Shirt
(melody: If You're Happy and You Know It)

Put your finger on your shirt, on your shirt.
Put your finger on your shirt, on your shirt.
Put your finger on your shirt,
Put your finger on your shirt,
Put your finger on your shirt, on your shirt.

On your shoes . . .

On your pants . . .

Round About

Round about, round about   *Circle baby's palm, back, or belly*
Sat a little hare.   *with finger.*
The puppies came and chased him   *Run fingers up arm, back, or belly.*
Right up there!   *Tickle under chin.*

Round and Round the Garden

Round and round the garden   *Circle baby's palm, back, or belly.*
Goes the teddy bear.
One step, two step,   *Walk fingers up arm, back, or chest.*
Tickle under there.   *Tickle under chin.*

Rub a Dub Dub

Rub a dub dub   *With baby on lap, rub baby's back*
Three men in a tub,   *or belly.*
And who do you think they be?
The butcher, the baker,   *Clap three times.*
The candlestick maker,
Throw 'em out,   *Lean back with baby and hug*
Knaves, all three!   *baby.*

Rub a Dub Dub, Who's in the Tub?

Rub a dub, dub,
Who's in the tub?
Little baby Matthew,
Scrub, scrub, scrub!

Shoe the Old Horse

Shoe the old horse,   *Tap baby's foot.*
Shoe the old mare,   *Tap baby's other foot.*
But let the little ponies
Run bare, bare, bare.   *Tap soles of feet together.*

These Are Baby's Fingers

These are baby's fingers,   *Touch baby's fingers.*
These are baby's toes.   *Touch baby's toes.*
This is baby's belly button,   *Circle baby's belly button.*
Round and round it goes.

This Little Pig

This little pig went to market   *Touch each of baby's fingers*
This little pig stayed home.   *or toes.*
This little pig had roast beef.
This little pig had none.
And this little pig cried,
"Wee, wee, wee," all the way home.   *Run fingers up baby's leg or arm.*

FOOD RHYMES

Baté, Baté, Chocolaté

Uno, dos, tres, cho,   *Count out with three fingers*
Uno, dos, tres, co,   *on each line.*
Uno, dos, tres, la,
Uno, dos, tres, té,
Baté, baté, chocolaté.   *Make stirrring motions.*

One, two, three, cho,
One, two, three, co,
One, two, three, la,
Stir, stir, chocolate.

Here Is a Doughnut

Here is a doughnut,   *Make a circle with four fingers*
Round and fat.   *and thumb.*
There's a hole   *Use finger of other hand to put*
In the middle   *inside the "hole."*
But you can't eat that!   *Shake head "no."*

Here's a Cup

Here's a cup   *Make circle with one hand.*
And here's a cup   *Make circle with other hand.*
And here's a pot of tea.   *Bring hands together in one big circle.*
Pour one cup,   *Pour one hand into the other.*
And pour the other cup.
And drink a cup with me.   *Petend to drink tea.*

Hot Cross Buns

Hot cross buns,
Hot cross buns,
One a penny, two a penny
Hot cross buns.

I Eat My Peas with Honey

I eat my peas with honey,   *Pat out rhythm on thighs.*
I've done it all my life.
I know it may seem funny,
But it keeps them on my knife!

I'm a Little Teapot

I'm a little teapot
Short and stout.
Here is my handle.   *One hand on hip.*
Here is my spout.   *The other arm out to side.*

When I get all steamed up,
Hear me shout.
Just tip me over and   *Tip over to "spout" side.*
Pour me out.

Milkman, Milkman

Milkman, milkman
Where have you been?
In Buttermilk Channel up to my chin.   *Touch baby's chin.*
I spilled my milk, and I spoiled my   *Rub baby's shirt.*
   clothes
And I got a long icicle hung from my   *Touch baby's nose.*
   nose.

Muffin Man

Oh, do you know the Muffin Man,
The Muffin Man, the Muffin Man?
Oh, do you know the Muffin Man,
Who lives on Drury Lane?

Oh, yes I know the Muffin Man,
The Muffin Man, the Muffin Man.
Oh, yes I know the Muffin Man.
He lives on Drury Lane.

Pancake

Mix a pancake, stir a pancake,   *Make stirring motions.*
Pop it in a pan.   *Clap on "pop."*
Fry a pancake, toss a pancake,   *Pretend to toss something up.*
Catch it if you can.   *Petend to catch.*

Pease Porridge Hot

Pease porridge hot,   *Clap hands in rhythm to the words.*
Pease porridge cold.
Pease porridge in the pot,
Nine days old.
Some like it hot,
Some like it cold,
And some like it in the pot,
Nine days old.

Polly Put the Kettle On

Polly put the kettle on.   *Pretend to hand something out.*
Polly put the kettle on.
Polly put the kettle on.
We'll all have tea.   *Make drinking motion.*

Sukey take it off again.   *Pretend to pick something up.*
Sukey take it off again.
Sukey take it off again.
They've all gone away.   *Wave goodbye.*

Wash the Dishes

Wash the dishes,   *Rub hands in circular motion.*
Wipe the dishes.
Ring the bell for tea.   *Pull imaginary string to ring bell.*
Three good wishes,   *Hold up three fingers.*
Three good kisses,   *Blow three kisses.*
I will give to thee.   *Point to baby.*

OUT AND ABOUT

Away up High (Baby)

Away up high in the apple tree,   *Lift baby up.*
I saw a little baby smiling at me.
I shook that tree as hard as I could.   *Shake baby gently.*
Down came the baby,   *Bring baby down for a hug.*
Mmm, was she good!   *Give baby a kiss.*

Away up High

Away up high in the apple tree,
I saw a little apple smiling at me.
I shook that tree as hard as I could.
Down came the apple,
Mmm, was it good!

Here's a Leaf

Here's a leaf,   *Hold palm out flat.*
And here's a leaf.   *Hold other palm out flat.*
And that makes two.   *Bring flat hands together, pinkies*
                                        touching.
Here's a bud   *Bring palms together.*
That makes a flower.   *Open hands, keep wrists touching.*
Watch it bloom for you!   *Raise hands slightly upward.*

I Hear Thunder
(melody: Frere Jaques)

I hear thunder, I hear thunder.   *Pretend to listen.*
Don't you, too? Don't you, too?   *Point to baby.*
Pitter-patter raindrops   *Make rain with fingers.*
Pitter-patter raindrops
I'm wet through,   *Point to self.*
So are you.   *Point to baby.*

The Itsy-Bitsy Spider

The itsy-bitsy spider
Went up the water spout.
Down came the rain
And washed the spider out.

Out came the sun,
And dried up all the rain.
And the itsy bitsy spider
Went up the spout again.

Let's Take a Walk

Let's take a walk,
Take a walk, take a walk,
To see what we can see.

Little Leaves
(melody: London Bridge)

Little leaves fall gently down,   *Stand up, have hands flutter down.*
Gently down, gently down,
Whirling, whirling, round and round,   *Turn around in place.*
Down, down, down.   *Stand up, have hands flutter down.*

London Bridge

London Bridge is falling down.
Falling down, falling down.
London Bridge is falling down.
My sweet baby.

Come and take a walk around,
Walk around, walk around.
Come and take a walk around,
My sweet baby.

Marching Song
(melody: If You're Happy and You Know it)

Let's all march down the street,   *Grownups and children hold hands*
Down the street.   *and walk around the circle.*
Let's all march down the street,
Down the street.
Let's all march down the street,
Smile at everyone we meet.
Let's all march down the street,
Down the street.

Mister Sun

Oh Mister Sun, Sun,   *Arms over head in a circle.*
Mister Golden Sun,
Please shine down on me.   *Point to self.*
Oh Mister Sun, Sun,   *Arms over head in a circle.*
Mister Golden Sun,
Hiding behind a tree.   *Hide face behind hands.*

These little children   *Point to children.*
Are asking you.
To please come out
So we can play with you.
Oh Mister Sun, Sun,   *Arms over head in a circle.*
Mister Golden Sun,
Please shine down on me.   *Point to self.*

The Rain

Pitter-patter, raindrops,   *Flutter fingers downward.*
Falling from the sky.
Here is my umbrella   *Hold hands, fingers touching,*
To keep me safe and dry.   *over head.*

When the rain is over
And the sun begins to glow,   *Make circle with arms over head.*
Little flowers start to bud   *Cup hands together.*
And grow and grow and grow.   *Spread hands out and upward.*

Rain on the Rooftops

Rain on the rooftops.   *Clap hands in rhythm to rhyme.*
Rain on the tree.
Rain on the green grass.
But not on me!

Rain, Rain Go Away

Rain, rain go away
Come again some other day.
Rain, rain go away.
All these children want to play.

Rain Is Falling Down

Rain is falling down—splash!
Rain is falling down—splash!
Rain is falling down—splash!
Pitter patter pitter patter,
Rain is falling down—splash!

Sun is peeking out—peek!
Sun is peeking out—peek!
Sun is peeking out—peek!
Peeking here,
Peeking there,
Sun is peeking out—peek!

Red Says Stop

Red says stop,
Green says go,
Yellow says wait,
You'd better go slow!

This Is My Garden

This is my garden,
I'll rake it with care.
And some flower seeds
I will plant there.
The sun will shine
And the rain will fall.
And my garden will grow.
Straight and tall.

To Market, To Market

To market, to market,
To buy a fat pig.
Home again, home again,
Jiggety, jig.
To market, to market,
To buy a fat hog,
Home again, home again,
Jiggety, jog.

LULLABIES

Hush-a-Bye

Hush-a-bye, don't you cry.
Go to sleepy, little baby.
When you wake, you shall have
All the pretty little horses.
Blacks and bays, dapples and grays,
All the pretty little horses.
Hush-a-bye, don't you cry.
Go to sleepy, little baby.

Lavender's Blue

Lavender's blue, dilly dilly,
Lavender's green.
When I am king, dilly dilly,
You shall be queen.

Who told you so, dilly dilly,
Who told you so.
'Twas my own heart, dilly dilly,
That told me so.

Roses are red, dilly dilly,
Violets are blue.
Because you love me, dilly dilly,
I will love you.

Who told you so, dilly dilly,
Who told you so.
'Twas my own heart, dilly dilly,
That told me so.

Rock-a-Bye Baby

Rock-a-bye baby.
On the tree top.
When the winds blow,
The cradle will rock.
When the bough breaks,
The cradle will fall.
And down will come baby,
Cradle and all.

See Saw Margery Daw

See saw Margery Daw
Baby loves when we hug him.
Baby has all the hugs in the world.
Because he knows we love him.

Star Light
(melody: Rain, Rain, Go Away)

Star light, star bright,   *"Twinkle" hands in the air.*
First star I see tonight,
I wish I may, I wish I might,
Have the wish I wish tonight.

Twinkle, Twinkle Little Star

Twinkle, twinkle little star,   *"Twinkle" hands in the air.*
How I wonder what you are.
Up above the world so high,
Like a diamond in the sky.   *Form hands to make a diamond shape.*
Twinkle, twinkle little star.
How I wonder what you are.

SPECIAL OCCASION RHYMES

Five Little Pumpkins

Five little pumpkins sitting on a gate.
The first one said, "Oh my it's getting late."
The second one said, "There are witches in the air."
The third one said, "But I don't care."
The fourth one said, "Let's run and run and run."
The fifth one said, "I'm ready for some fun."
Oooh went the wind and out went the light.
And the five little pumpkins rolled out of sight.

Jack O'Lantern

A face so round
And eyes so bright
A nose that glows
My, what a sight!
A fiery mouth
With jolly grin
No arms no legs
Just stem to chin.

Jack O'Lantern II

Carve a jack-o-lantern
On Halloween night.
He has a big mouth,
But he doesn't bite.
He has two big eyes,
But he cannot see.
He's a funny jack o'lantern
As happy as can be.

I Have a Little Heart

I have a little heart
That goes thump, thump, thump.
It keeps right on beating
As I jump, jump, jump.

I get a special feeling
When I look at you.
So I'll blow you a kiss
Or two.

Valentines

Valentines, valentines,
Valentines true.
I'll find a nice one
And give it to you.

Flowers are sweet
This is true,
But for my valentine
I choose you!

5

PUPPET RHYMES

The puppets featured in the programs in this book are Folkmanis puppets. They have been making puppets of all kinds and sizes for many years. Their website is *www.folkmanis.com* and you can view many of the puppets mentioned in this book. They are always producing new puppets and discontinuing others, so you'll always have an opportunity to add to your collection and rhyme repertoire. Some additional puppet rhymes not used in the programs are contained in this section.

PUPPET RHYME LIST

The Squirrel
Three White Mice in a Red Box
Bluebirds in Nest
Little Frog
Turtle
Three Chicks
The Bee
Baby Bumble Bee
Redbirds
Three Birds
Three Bunnies

Three Pigs
Mouse in Cheese
Puppies in Basket

Monkey Mitt Rhymes
Five Kittens in the Bed
Five Little Monkeys
Redbirds II
Frogs
Flowers

The Squirrel

Here's my friend
He's a squirrel brown
With a fluffy tail
And ears so round.

Do you like his home?
It's a tree that's brown
And he has a window
To look around.

We'll say goodbye
He's going inside.
But he'll come back out
When we call on him next time.

Three White Mice in a Red Box

My red box is a present
But it isn't what you think
There are three little friends inside
With noses that are pink.

Can you guess what they are?
They're three white mice!
With their long white tails
Don't they look nice?

But they like their home
As you can see
They're going back in
So say goodbye, 1-2-3!

Bluebirds in Nest
(melody: Bluebird, Bluebird found in *Preschool Songs*)

Bluebird, bluebird,
Through my window,
Bluebird, bluebird,
Through my window,
Bluebird, bluebird,
Through my window,
Oh Mommy I am happy.

Little Frog

A little frog in a pond am I.
Hippity, hippity, hop.
And I can jump in the air, so high!
Hippity, hippity, hop.

Turtle

This is my turtle
He lives in his shell
He pokes his head out
When he wants to eat
But he pulls it back
When he wants to sleep!

Three Chicks

Three white chicks in a basket brown
Who pop up their heads to look around
They bow their heads to say hello
Let's count them now before they go.

How many are there?
Well, let's see
Help me count them
One-two-three.

Now wave good-bye
As they lay down
And go to sleep
In their basket brown.

The Bee

The bee loves his pretty pink flower
He visits every day.
He gathers sweet nectar for honey
That's why he likes to stay.

Baby Bumble Bee
(If sung, use melody in *More Tickles and Tunes*)

I'm bringing home a baby bumble bee.
Won't my mommy be so proud of me?
I'm bringing home a baby bumble bee.
Bzz, bzz, bzz, says the bumble bee.

Redbirds

Here are the redbirds,
Tra, la, la, la la.
Here are the redbirds,
Tra, la, la, la, la.
Snug in their nest.
(Or bluebirds, blackbirds, whitebirds, etc.)

Three Birds

Three little birds in a warm snug nest
They stretch their wings, then go back for a rest
They stay right here and never fly
Just wave their wings to say hi.
(Depending on their color, you can change the word little to blue, red, or
brown, etc.)

Three Bunnies

Three little bunnies in a basket green
They're hopping up and down
So happy to be seen.
If you wave to them, they'll say hi.
And when they're tired of hopping,
They'll say good-bye.

Three Pigs

One little, two little, three little piggies,
Living in their house are three little piggies,
Little and pink and soft are the piggies,
Living in their house.

Mouse in Cheese
(If sung, use melody for Rain Is Falling Down in "The Baby Record")

Where's the baby mouse? Squeak!
See his special house? Squeak!
Here's his head! Squeak!
Gone to bed! Squeak!
Where's the baby mouse? Squeak!

Puppies in Basket
(If sung, use melody of A Tisket, a Tasket found in *Here is Thumbkin*)

A tisket, a tasket,
The puppies in their basket
They wave their heads to say, hello.
From in their cozy basket.

MONKEY MITTS

Monkey mitts are gloves that are usually either furry or black cloth. The tip of each finger is sticky and a small puppet or figure can be attached to it. They are often sold as sets with various figures contained in the set. Some tell a story like the Three Little Kittens or invite a particular song like *Old MacDonald,* but many are just five of something, whether they are monkeys or rabbits or frogs or ducks. You can find them in many catalogs, as well as websites, including *www.beyondplay.com* and *www.shopbecker.com.*

MONKEY MITT RHYMES

Five Kittens in the Bed
(If sung, use the melody, Roll Over, found in *Toddler Tunes.*)

Five kittens in the bed
And the little one said,
"I'm crowded, roll over."
So they all rolled over
And one fell out
(Continue for four, three, and two.)

One kitten in the bed,
And the little one said,
"I'm lonely."
So they all jumped in
And the little one said,
"All right, good night!"

Five Little Monkeys

Five little monkeys jumping on the bed,
One fell off and bumped his head.
Mamma called the doctor and the doctor said,
"No more monkeys jumping on the bed."
(Repeat for four, three, two and one.)

Redbirds II

Here are the redbirds,
Tra, la, la, la, la.
Here are the redbirds,
Tra, la, la, la, la.
Watch one fly away.
(Or bluebirds, blackbirds, whitebirds, etc.)

Frogs

Here are froggies, hippety-hop
With a hop
And a Stop
And a hop
And a stop!

Flowers

(If sung, use Frere Jaques found in *Toddler Favorites*)

Five little flowers are standing in the sun,
See their heads nodding, bowing one by one.
Down, down, down falls the gentle rain.
Five little flowers lift their heads again.

APPENDIX: RESOURCES

RHYME AND SONG COLLECTIONS

Animal Crackers: A Delectable Collection of Pictures, Poems and Lullabies for the Very Young. Collected and illustrated by Jane Dyer. Boston: Little Brown, 1996.

The Annotated Mother Goose: Nursery Rhymes Old and New. Arranged and explained by William Baring-Gould and Cecil Baring-Gould. Illustrated by Caldecott et al. New York: Clarkson-Potter, Inc., 1982.

Arroz con Leche: Popular Songs and Rhymes from Latin America. Illustrated by Lulu Delacre. New York: Scholastic, 1989.

The Baby's Game Book. Selected by Isabel Wilner. Illustrated by Sam Williams. New York: Greenwillow Books/HarperCollins, 2000.

The Candlewick Book of First Rhymes. Illustrated by Maurice Sendak, Helen Oxenbury, et. al. Cambridge, MA: Candlewick Press, 1996.

A Child's Book of Lullabies. Compiled by Shona McKellar. Paintings by Mary Cassatt. New York: DK Publishing, Inc., 1997.

A Child's Treasury of Nursery Rhymes. Illustrated by Kady MacDonald Denton. New York: Kingfisher, 1998.

Eye Winker, Tom Tinker, Chin Chopper: Fifty Musical Fingerplays. Tom Glazer. Illustrated by Ron Himler. Garden City: Doubleday, 1973.

Here Comes Mother Goose. Edited by Iona Opie. Illustrated by Rosemary Wells. Cambridge, MA: Candlewick Press, 1999.

Jane Yolen's Mother Goose Songbook. Edited by Jane Yolen. Illustrated by Rosekrans Hoffman. Musical arrangements by Adam Stemple. Honesdale, PA: Boyds Mill Press, 1992.

Knock at the Door and other Baby Action Rhymes. Kay Chorao. New York: Dutton Children's Books, 1999.

The Lucy Cousins Book of Nursery Rhymes. Collected and illustrated by Lucy Cousins. New York: Dutton Children's Books, 1999.

Lullabies. An Illustrated Songbook. Music arranged by Richard Kapp. New York, San Diego: Metropolitan Museum of Art, Gulliver Books/Harcourt Brace, 1997.

Mother Goose Remembers. Clare Beaton. New York: Barefoot Books, 2000.

The Mother Goose Songbook. Selected and adapted by Tom Glazer. Illustrated by David McPhail. New York: Doubleday, 1990.

The Movable Mother Goose. Illustrated by Robert Sabuda. New York: Little Simon, 1999.

My Very First Mother Goose. Edited by Iona Opie. Illustrated by Rosemary Wells. Cambridge, MA: Candlewick Press, 1996.

The Orchard Book of Nursery Rhymes. Compiled by Zena Sutherland. Illustrated by Faith Jacques. New York: Orchard Books, 1990.

Ring A Ring 'o Roses. Finger Plays for Pre-school Children. Tenth Edition. Flint, MI: Flint Public Library, 1996.

Shake it to the One that You Love the Best: Play Songs and Lullabies from Black Musical Traditions. Collected and adapted by Cheryl Warren Mattox. With illustrations from works of Varnette P. Honeywood and Brenda Joysmith. Nashville, Tenn: JTC of Nashville, 1989.

Songs from Mother Goose: with the Traditional Melody for Each. Compiled by Nancy Larrick. Illustrated by Robin Spowart. New York: Harper & Row, 1989.

A Stitch in Rhyme: A Nursery Rhymes Sampler with Embroidered Illustrations. Illustrated by Belinda Downes. New York: Alfred Knopf: Distributed by Random House, 1996.

Sylvia Long's Mother Goose. Illustrated by Sylvia Long. San Francisco: Chronicle Books, 1999.

Tortillitas Para Mama and Other Nursery Rhymes/Spanish and English. Selected and translated by Margo C. Griego et al. Illustrated by Barbara Cooney. New York: Holt, Rinehart & Winston, 1981.

Twilight Verses, Moonlight Rhymes. Compiled by Mary Joslin. Illustrated by Liz Pichon. Minneapolis, MN: Augsburg, 1999.

INFANT PICTURE BOOKS

Prewalker Books

All The Pretty Little Horses. A Traditional Lullaby. Illustrated by Linda Saport. New York: Clarion, 1999. *This classic, familiar folksong is given a new life here, with beautiful impressionist illustrations juxtaposed with the lyrics. Sing it or say it.*

Brown, Margaret Wise. *Goodnight Moon.* Illustrated by Clement Hurd. New York: Harper & Row, 1947. *With its now familiar palette of red, green, and gold and familiar goodnights to all things important to baby, this is a classic of infancy and bedtime.*

Charlip, Remy. *Baby Hearts & Baby Flowers.* New York: HarperCollins, 2002. *With simple phrases on each page and soft, pastel illustrations, this is a perfect prewalker book and a perfect goodnight book.*

Gentieu, Penny. *Baby! Talk!* New York: Crown Publishers, 1999. *With little text but lots of photos of adorable babies, this is always a winner.*

Henderson, Kathy. *The Baby's Book of Babies.* Photographs by Anthea Sieveking. New York: Dial Books for Young Readers, 1989. *Babies who are eating, washing, and squashing the shopping; they are everywhere!*

———. *Bounce, Bounce, Bounce.* Illustrated by Carol Thompson. Cambridge, MA: Candlewick Press, 1994. *A lilting rhyming text is the highlight of this fun, action-packed book.*

———. *Bumpety, Bump.* Illustrated by Carol Thompson. Cambridge, MA: Candlewick Press, 1994. *The perfect partner to* Bounce, Bounce, Bounce, *this one uses lots of verbs and humor in its spare, wry text.*

Marzollo, Jean. *Mama Mama.* Illustrated by Laura Regan. Harper Growing Tree. New York: HarperFestival, 1999. *A board book that sings the praises of mother's love in all kinds of animals.*

Taylor, Ann. *Baby Dance.* Illustrated by Marjorie Van Heerden. Harper Growing Tree. New York: HarperFestival, 1999. *Baby and Daddy find all kinds of ways to swoop high, low, and around as they dance around the house.*

Thomas, Joyce Carol. *You Are My Perfect Baby.* Illustrated by Nneka Bennett. Harper Growing Tree. New York: HarperFestival, 1999. *An ode to every little part of baby, from nose to toes, and all of it perfect.*

Tracy, Tom. *Show Me!* Illustrated by Darcia Labrosse. Harper Growing Tree. New York: HarperFestival, 1999. *With its question and answer format, the reading is an interactive experience.*

Wardlaw, Lee. *First Steps.* Illustrated by Julie Paschkis. Harper Growing Tree. New York: HarperFestival, 1999. *An important moment in every baby's life is celebrated here.*

Weiss, Nicki. *Where Does the Brown Bear Go?* New York: Greenwillow, 1989. *All the animals are "on their way home," in this classic, rhyming text that puts baby and all the animals to sleep.*

Walker Books

Apperly, Dawn. *Good Night, Sleep Tight, Little Bunnies.* New York: Scholastic, 2002. *One by one, each of the animals goes to sleep. And what do we say to them? Good night, sleep tight!*

Berry, Holly. *Busy Lizzie.* New York: North-South Books, 1994. *Lizzie is very busy, as she kicks her feet, claps her hands, tugs her ears, and goes to sleep in her big girl bed.*

Big Fat Hen. Illustrated by Keith Baker. San Diego: Harcourt Brace & Co., 1994. *In slightly oversized format, a brightly illustrated version of "One, two, buckle my shoe" that is fun to read out loud.*

Boynton, Sandra. *Pajama Time!* New York: Workman Pub., 2000. *It's a rollicking, dancing, prancing good time! Why? It's pajama time!*

Deming, A. G. *Who is Tapping at My Window?* Illustrated by Monica Wellington. New York: Dutton, 1988. *Is it the pony, or the mouse tapping on baby's window? No, it's the rain, tapping on the windowpane.*

Fleming, Denise. *Barnyard Banter.* New York: Henry Holt, 1994. *Lots of crowing, mooing, and clucking will fill the air as you go down to the barnyard.*

———. *In the Small, Small Pond.* New York: Henry Holt, 1993. *Who lives in the pond? What do they do? Find out in this journey to the land of frogs, beavers, and birds.*

———. *In the Tall, Tall Grass.* New York: Henry Holt, 1991. *Bats swoop, beetles hurry, snakes glide. There are lots of critters hiding in the grass. Baby will love to spot them in the colorful, cut-paper collage illustrations.*

Fox, Mem. *Time for Bed.* Illustrated by Jane Dyer. San Diego: Harcourt Brace & Co., 1993. *A soothing, rhyming goodnight ode to all the animal babies from their mamas. For the fish, the birds, even the snakes, it's "time for bed."*

George, Kristine O'Connell. *Book!* Illustrated by Maggie Smith. New York: Clarion, 2001. *What is a great gift that goes anywhere and doubles as a playmate? It's a book! A great read-aloud.*

Greenfield, Eloise. *Water Water.* Illustrated by Jan Spivey Gilchrist. Harper Growing Tree. New York: HarperFestival, 1999. *From the water in the sink to the rain, rivers, and seas, water is everywhere. There's even good water "in my cup."*

Hubbell, Patricia. *Pots and Pans.* Illustrated by Diane DeGroat. Harper Growing Tree. New York: HarperFestival, 1998. *A repetitive rhyming text and differing fonts makes this book a whirlwind experience.*

Kamen, Gloria. *"Paddle," Said the Swan.* New York: Atheneum, 1989. *This book's rhythm makes it a lovely read-aloud. Its list of animals and their sounds make this a toddler favorite.*

Katz, Karen. *Counting Kisses.* Margaret K. McElderry Books, 2001. *From ten to one, how many kisses does baby get from her head to her toes? Lots and lots.*

Maitland, Barbara. *My Bear and Me.* Illustrated by Lisa Flather. New York: Margaret K. McEderry Books, 1999. *A little girl tells about her best friend, as they sing, swing, and do everything together.*

Martin, Bill & John Archambault. *Here Are My Hands.* Illustrated by Ted Rand. New York: Henry Holt, 1987. *A classic story for toddlers, as everything from hands, to feet, to head is recounted for what they can do.*

Martin, Bill. *Brown Bear, Brown Bear, What Do You See?* Illustrated by Eric Carle. New York: Henry Holt, 1992. *A wonderful combination of animals and colors that toddlers and their caregivers love. Each page asks a question that's answered on the next page.*

McDonnell, Flora. *I Love Animals.* Cambridge, MA: Candlewick Press, 1994. *A slightly oversized format with large illustrations of animals that fill the pages accompany an accessible, rhyming text.*

———. *I Love Boats.* Cambridge, MA: Candlewick Press, 1995. *With essentially the same format as the animals book, these bright, large boats fill the pages of this book until they end up—in the tub!*

McGee, Marni. *Sleepy Me.* Illustrated by Sam Williams. New York: Simon & Schuster Books for Young Readers, 2001. *Listen to all the sleepy sounds inside and outside the house as baby goes to sleep.*

Meyers, Susan. *Everywhere Babies.* Illustrated by Marla Frazee. San Diego: Harcourt, 2001. *Babies and all that they do, accompanied by illustrations of adorable tots, makes this an irresistible choice.*

Ray, Karen. *Sleep Song.* Illustrated by Rhonda Mitchell. New York: Orchard Books, 1995. *A rhythmic rhyming journey a little one takes from play to sleep.*

Seuling, Barbara. *Winter Lullaby.* Illustrated by Greg Newbold. San Diego: Browndeer Press/Harcourt Brace & Co., 1998. *As the weather gets cold, all of nature tucks up for a long winter's nap. A perfect accompaniment to baby's sleep time.*

Siomades, Lorianne. *The Itsy Bitsy Spider.* Honesdale, PA: Boyds Mill Press, 1999. *A simple version of this well-known rhyme, with one phrase on each page and bright, colorful illustrations.*

Spowart, Robin. *Ten Little Bunnies.* New York: Scholastic, 2001. *Warm, round, fuzzy illustrations capture these adorable bunnies as they help Daddy, eat ice cream, or swing. Let's count them one to ten!*

Sturges, Philemon. *I Love Trucks.* Illustrated by Shari Halpern. New York: HarperCollins, 1999. *This will be a hit with every truck lover. Every truck, from steamroller to ice cream truck, is catalogued in this fast-paced, fun text.*

Titherington, Jeanne. *Baby's Boat.* New York: Greenwillow, 1992. *A gentle lullaby in a book form with lavender-hued illustrations showing baby in his boat drifting off to dreamland.*

Wood, Don and Audrey. *Piggies.* Illustrated by Don Wood. San Diego: Harcourt Brace Jovanovich, 1991. *Humor abounds in this silly story about all of babies' "piggies."*

Young, Ruth. *Golden Bear.* Illustrated by Rachel Isadora. New York: Viking, 1992. *Nothing's more special than Golden Bear, this young boy's favorite friend.*

MUSIC RECORDINGS

The songs indicated with each recording are songs used in the programs in this book. Each recording has many other wonderful songs for you to use.

Buchman, Rachel. *Baby and Me.* Albany, NY: Gentle Wind, 1999. *Round and Round the Garden; Clap Hands! Clap Hands!*

Capon, Jack & Rosemary Hallum. *Children's All-Time Rhythm Favorites.* Freeport, N.Y.: Educational Activities, 1994. *If You're Happy and You Know it.*

Cassidy, Nancy. *KidsSongs.* Palo Alto, CA: KLUTZ, 1986. *Mister Sun, Twinkle, Twinkle Little Star.*

———. *KidSongs2.* Palo Alto, CA: KLUTZ, 1986. *Lavender's Blue, Head and Shoulders.*

Cedarmont Kids Singers. *Preschool Songs. 22 Classic Songs for Kids.* Franklin, TN: Nashville, TN: Cedarmont Music, 1995. *Down by the Station; Bluebird, Bluebird; Where is Thumbkin? Head, Shoulders, Knees and Toes; Ring Around the Rosy.*

———. *Toddler Tunes. 25 Classic Songs for Toddlers.* Franklin, TN: Cedarmont Music, 1994. *The Wheels on the Bus; Polly Put the Kettle On; Eensy, Weensy*

Spider; Mulberry Bush; Baa, Baa, Black Sheep; Jack and Jill; London Bridge; Mary Had a Little Lamb; The Muffin Man; Row, Row, Row Your Boat; Roll Over.

Feierabend, John and Luann Saunders. *Round and Round the Garden. Music in My First Year.* Chicago: GIA Publications, Inc., 2000. *Ride a Cock Horse; To Market, to Market; Rock-a-Bye; Rain, Rain Go Away; These are Baby's Fingers; Round and Round the Garden; Pat-a-Cake; Shoe the Horse; Shoe the Colt; Handy Spandy; Seesaw, Margery Daw; Hot Cross Buns.*

———. *Ride Away on Your Horses. Music Now I'm One.* Chicago: GIA Publications, Inc., 2000. *Leg over Leg, Seesaw Margery Daw, Ring Around the Rosy, Roly Poly, Round and Round the Garden, Clap Your Hands, From Wibbleton to Wobbleton.*

———. *Frog in the Meadow. Music Now I'm Two!* Chicago: GIA Publications, Inc., 2000. *Mother and Father and Uncle John; Trot Trot to Boston; This is the Way the Ladies Ride; Tommy O'Flynn; The Mulberry Bush.*

Hammett, Carol Totsky & Elaine Bueffel. *Toddlers on Parade. Musical Exercise for Infants and Toddlers.* Long Branch, NJ: Kimbo Educational, 1985. *Grand Old Duke of York; Roll Your Hands; Wheels on the Bus; Ride a Cock Horse.*

Hegner, Priscilla. *Baby Games.* Long Branch, NJ: Kimbo, 1987. *Say, Say Oh Baby; Hush Little Baby.*

Here is Thumbkin! More Action Songs for Every Month. Long Branch, NJ: Kimbo Educational, 2000. *Hush Little Baby; Down by the Station; A Tisket A Tasket.*

Jenkins, Ella. *Ella Jenkins Nursery Rhymes.* Washington DC: Smithsonian Folkways, 1990. *Muffin Man, The Mulberry Bush, Humpty Dumpty, This Little Piggy, Pease Porridge Hot.*

———. *Early Early Childhood Songs.* Washington D.C: Smithsonian Folkways, 1990. *Mary Had a Little Lamb, Skip to My Lou, Twinkle, Twinkle Little Star, London Bridge (all instrumental).*

Lullaby: A Collection. Produced by Leib Ostrow. Redway, CA: Music for Little People. Distributed by Warner Brothers, 1994. *All the Pretty Little Horses.*

McGrath, Bob & Katherine Smithrim. *The Baby Record.* Teaneck, NJ: Bob's Kids Music, 2000. *Baby a Go Go; Come a Look a See; Riding on My Pony; Starlight, Starbright; What Do I Do with My Baby-O? Tommy O'Flynn, This Little Pig, Rickety, Rickety, Rocking Horse, Round and Round the Garden, These Are Baby's Fingers, Shoe the Old Horse, Clap Your Hands Little Sally, Rain Is Falling Down.*

———. *If You're Happy and You Know It. Sing Along with Bob McGrath,* Vol. 1. Toronto, ON: Kids' Records, 1984. *If You're Happy and You Know it; Baa Baa Black Sheep; Wheels on the Bus; Skip to My Lou; Incey Wincey Spider; Where is Thumbkin?; Mr. Sun; Looby Loo.*

———. *Songs & Games for Toddlers*. Teaneck, NJ: Bob's Kids Records, 2000. *Twinkle, Twinkle, Little Star; Frere Jacques; Row, Row, Row Your Boat, Teddy Bear, Teddy Bear*.

Mediterranean Lullaby. Roslyn, NY: Ellipsis Arts, 2000. *A collection of lullabies from countries around the world, including songs from Greece, Lebanon, and Spain*.

Mollin, Fred. *Disney's Lullaby Album*. Burbank, CA: Walt Disney Records, 2000. *Twinkle, Twinkle Little Star*.

Mozart, Wolfgang Amadeus. *Mozart for Babies. Awake Time*. Los Angeles: Rhino, 1998. *A selection of excerpts and short pieces, all done with light and gentle orchestration*.

———. *Mozart for Babies. Sleepy Time*. Los Angeles: Rhino, 1998. *A selection of excerpts and short pieces, all done with light and gentle orchestration, using "baby-friendly" instruments*.

Music Workshop for Kids. *Sleeping with the Fishes*. Minneapolis, MN: Baby Music Boom, 1997. *Twinkle, Twinkle Little Star; Hush Little Baby*.

Oppenheimer, Matt. *A Gentle African Journey*. Los Angeles, CA: Kid Rhino, 1998. *Lovely music, and some singing, that will be sure to lull baby to sleep*.

Palmer, Hap. *A Child's World of Lullabies: Multicultural Songs for Quiet Times*. Topanga, CA: Hap-Pal Music, 1993. *Hush Little Baby*

———. *Hap Palmer Sings Classic Nursery Rhymes*. Freeport, NY: Educational Activities, 1991. *Ride a Cock Horse; Mary Had a Little Lamb; Humpty Dumpty*.

Playtime Activity Songs to Share with Your Baby. Burbank, CA: Disney, 1991. *Itsy Bitsy Spider; Wheels on the Bus; Where is Thumbkin? I'm a Little Teapot, Hickory, Dickory, Dock; This is the Way the Ladies Ride*.

Raffi. *Singable Songs Collection*. Compilation of *Singable Songs for the Very Young, More Singable Songs, Corner Grocery Store*. Vancouver, B.C.: Shoreline Records, 1996. *Baa Baa Black Sheep; Mr. Sun; Frere Jacques, Rock-a-Bye, Baby*.

Raffi. *Raffi's Box of Sunshine*. Compilation of *Rise and Shine; One Light, One Sun; Everything Grows*, Willowdale, ON: Shoreline Records, 2000. *Wheels on the Bus; Twinkle, Twinkle Little Star, Row, Row, Row Your Boat*.

Reid-Naiman, Kathy. *More Tickles & Tunes*. Aurora, ON.: Merriweather Records, 1997. *Bumble Bee, Open/Shut Them, Leg Over Leg, Ride a Cock Horse; This is the Way; The Grand Old Duke of York*.

———. *Say Hello to the Morning. More Tickles, Tunes and Singing Games for Children*. Aurora, ON: Merriweather Records, 1999. *Kangaroo Brown, Seesaw Margery Daw*.

———. *Tickles and Tunes. Tickles, Songs and Bounces for Children 6 Months to 6 Years Old*. Aurora, ON: Merriweather Records, 1994. *Skip to My Lou; Baby-O; To Market, To Market; Trit, Trot to Boston; Humpty-Dumpty*.

Stewart, Georgiana Liccione. *Baby Face. Activities for Infants and Toddlers.* Long Branch, NJ: Kimbo Educational, 1983. *Ring Around the Rosie; Rock-a-Bye Baby.*

———. *Get a Good Start.* Long Branch, NJ: Kimbo, 1980. *If You're Happy and You Know It; Looby Loo; Frere Jacques; Twinkle, Twinkle Little Star.*

———. *Nursery Rhyme Time. Songs, Rhymes and Movement Activities.* Long Branch, NJ: Kimbo Educational, 2000. *Humpty Dumpty; Mulberry Bush; Baa Baa Black Sheep; Eensy Weensy Spider; Jack and Jill; Mary Had a Little Lamb; Twinkle, Twinkle Little Star; Rock-a-Bye Baby; Ring Around the Rosie.*

Storytime Favorites. Redway, CA: Los Angeles, CA: Music for Little People, Distributed by Kid Rhino, 2000. *Itsy Bitsy Spider; Jack and Jill; Mary Had a Little Lamb; Baa Baa Black Sheep; Muffin Man; Polly Put the Kettle On; Hush Little Baby; Twinkle, Twinkle Little Star.*

Toddler Favorites. Redway, CA: Music for Little People, 1998. *I'm a Little Teapot; The Wheels on the Bus; Where is Thumbkin?; Mary Had a Little Lamb; Skip to my Lou; Frere Jacques; Ring Around the Rosy; If You're Happy and You Know it; Baa Baa Black Sheep; Twinkle, Twinkle Little Star.*

Where is Thumbkin? Long Branch, NJ: Kimbo Educational, 1996. *Where is Thumbkin? If You're Happy and You Know it; Head, Shoulders, Knees and Toes; Open, Shut Them.*

Wiseman, Wendy. *Animal Nursery Rhyme Time.* Swanton, VT: Kidzup Productions Inc., 1996. *Eensy Weensy Spider; Ride a Cock Horse; Hickory, Dickory Dock; This Little Piggy.*

Wiseman, Wendy & Sari Dajani. *Best Toddler Tunes.* Swanton, VT: Kidzup Production Inc., 1999. *The Wheels on the Bus; Eensy Weensy Spider; Hickory Dickory Dock.*

Wiseman, Wendy. *Sleepy Time Rock-a-Byes.* Kidzup, 1996. *Twinkle Twinkle Little Star; Rock-a-Bye Baby; Frere Jacques; Baa Baa Black Sheep; Hush Little Baby.*

VIDEOS

Jaeger, Sally. *Mr. Bear says Hello.* Toronto: 49 North Productions, 2000. Sally Jaeger conducts a walker program, using such songs as *Ten Little Gentlemen, Rain is Falling Down,* and others.

Jaeger, Sally. *From Wibbleton to Wobbleton.* Toronto: 49 North Productions, 1998. Sally Jaeger conducts a lap baby program, using such songs as *Let's Take a Walk; Riding On My Pony; What Do We Do with the Baby-O? Bye Low My Baby; Go to Sleepy Baby-Bye.*

Mommy Songs Everyone Can Sing. Stargate Productions, 1995. Beth Corwin sings baby songs such as *Wheels on the Bus; Where is Thumbkin?; If You're Happy and You Know It; Itsy-Bitsy Spider; Row, Row, Row Your Boat; Twinkle, Twinkle Little Star. A good substitute for a library baby program for a baby and parent who are at home.*

BOARD BOOKS

Since so many of these titles are part of a series, the rest of the series' titles are listed below the primary title.

Ahlberg, Janet. *Baby Sleeps.* Boston: Little Brown & Co., 1998. (Also: *Blue Buggy, See the Rabbit, Doll and Teddy.*)

Barton, Byron. *Boats.* New York: HarperFestival, 1986. (Also: *Planes, Trains, Trucks.*)

Brown, Margaret Wise. *Goodnight Moon.* Illustrated by Clement Hurd. New York: Harper & Row, 1947. (Board Book edition, HarperFestival, 1996).

———. *Big Red Barn.* Illustrated by Felicia Bond. New York: HarperFestival, 1995.

———. *Runaway Bunny.* Illustrated by Clement Hurd. New York: Harper-Collins, 1991.

Carle, Eric. *From Head to Toe.* New York: HarperFestival, 1999.

Cousins, Lucy. *Where Does Maisy Live?* Cambridge, MA: Candlewick Press, 2000. (Also: *Count with Maisy* and *Maisy's Colors.*)

Cummings, Pat. *Purrrrr.* New York: Harper Growing Tree, HarperFestival, 1999.

Curious George's Are You Curious? Illustrated by H. A. Rey. Boston: Houghton Mifflin & Co., 1998. (Also: *Curious George's Opposites.*)

Demarest, Chris L. *Winter.* New York: Harcourt Brace & Co., 1996. (Also: *Fall, Spring, Summer.*)

Ehlert, Lois. *Color Zoo.* New York: HarperFestival, 1997. (Also: *Color Farm.*)

Hughes, Shirley. *Playing.* New York: HarperFestival, 1997. (*Also Being Together.*)

Hurd, Thacher. *Zoom City.* New York: Harper Growing Tree, HarperFestival, 1998.

Hutchins, Pat. *Rosie's Walk.* New York: Little Simon, 1998.

Martin, Bill. *Here Are My Hands.* New York: Henry Holt, 1998.

Marzollo, Jean. *Do You Know New?* Illustrated by Mari Takabayashi. New York: Harper Growing Tree, HarperFestival, 1998.

Miller, Margaret. *Baby Faces.* New York: Little Simon, 1998. (Also: *What's on My Head.*)

Opie, Iona. ed. *Wee Willie Winkie: and Other Rhymes*. Illustrated by Rosemary Wells. Cambridge, MA: Candlewick Press, 1997. (Also: *Pussycat Pussycat: and Other Rhymes. Little Boy Blue: and Other Rhymes. Humpty Dumpty: and Other Rhymes.*)

Oxenbury, Helen. *Tom and Pippo Go for a Walk*. New York: Little Simon, 1998. (Also: *Tom and Pippo Read a Story, Tom and Pippo's Day.*)

Tafuri, Nancy. *I Love You, Little One*. New York: Scholastic Press, 1998.

Taylor, Ann. *Baby Dance*. Illustrated by Marjorie van Heerden. New York: HarperFestival, 1999. (Harper Growing Tree Series.)

Titherington, Jeanne. *Baby's Boat*. New York: Greenwillow Press, 1998.

Weiss, Nicki. *Where Does the Brown Bear Go?* New York: Greenwillow Press, 1998.

Wells, Rosemary. *Max's New Suit*. New York: Dial Books for Young Readers, 1998. (Also: *Max's First Word, Max's Breakfast, Max's Birthday, Max's Toys, Max's Ride.*)

BABY'S BOOKSHELF

Brown, Margaret Wise. *Goodnight Moon*. Illustrated by Clement Hurd. Harper & Row, 1947. *A classic of infancy, this book is available in every format imaginable. Its simple text is a tribute to love between mother and baby. It's an indispensable addition.*

Burningham, John. *First Steps: Letters, Numbers, Colors, Opposites*. Cambridge, MA: Candlewick Press, 1994. *An introduction to letters, numbers, colors, and concepts.*

Carle, Eric. *The Very Hungry Caterpillar*. New York: Philomel Books, 1969. *The integration of colors, numbers, days of the week, and food items in a seamless story make this a perfect read, aloud choice.*

Fleming, Denise. *The Everything Book*. New York: Henry Holt, 2000. *A collection of simple stories and concepts, illustrated with cut-paper collage illustrations.*

Hopkins, Lee Bennett. *Climb into My Lap. First Poems to Read Together*. Illustrated by Kathryn Brown. New York: Simon & Schuster, 1998. *A charming collection of baby friendly poems that will provide hours of pleasure and delight.*

Hughes, Shirley. *Let's Join In: Four Stories*. Cambridge, MA: Candlewick Press, 1999. *Contents were previously published for short picture books: Hiding, Giving, Chatting and Bouncing. They are filled with charm and delight, as these four concepts are woven into stories.*

Kunhardt, Dorothy. *Pat the Bunny*. New York: Golden Books, 1940. *The first tactile book that is still a favorite baby gift.*

Martin, Bill. *Brown Bear, Brown Bear, What Do You See?* Illustrated by Eric Carle. New York: Henry Holt, 1983. *This rhyming, lilting classic combines the delight of guessing, the fun of colors, and the comfort of repetition. Read it, chant it, or sing it. Babies will love it.*

Opie, Iona. *My Very First Mother Goose.* Illustrated by Rosemary Wells. Cambridge, MA: Candlewick Press, 1996. (Also *Here Comes Mother Goose.*) *These are two wonderful collections of classic nursery rhymes, illustrated with adorable child and animal figures cavorting through the pages. Save a place for these on your shelf.*

Prelutsky, Jack. *Read-Aloud Rhymes for the Very Young.* With an introduction by Jim Trelease. Illustrated by Marc Brown. New York: A. Knopf, 1986. *A classic collection put together by three experts who know very young children and what they like to hear.*

Stories and Fun for the Very Young. Cambridge, MA: Candlewick Press, 1998. *A collection of twenty-five stories and rhymes for the very young, including works by Helen Oxenbury, Anthony Browne, and Rosemary Wells.*

Weiss, Nicki. *Where Does the Brown Bear Go?* New York: Greenwillow Press, 1989. *From its black pages with white text and the round, soft animals figures that prance through its landscape, to its gentle rhyming text, this is another bedtime classic.*

PROGRAMMING BOOKS
FINGER PLAY COLLECTIONS
PROFESSIONAL RESOURCES

Briggs, Diane. *52 Programs for Preschoolers:* the librarian's year-round planner. Chicago: American Library Association, 1997.

Cooper, Kay. *Neal-Schuman Index to Finger Plays.* New York: Neal Schuman, 1993.

Cooper, Kay. *Too Many Rabbits and other Fingerplays about Animals, Nature, Weather, and the Universe.* Illustrated by Judith Moffatt. New York: Scholastic, 1995.

The Eensty-Weensty Spider: Fingerplays and Action Rhymes. Selected by Joanna Cole and Stephanie Calmenson. Illustrated by Alan Tiegreen. New York: Morrow Junior Books, 1991.

Ernst, Linda L. *Lapsit Services for the Very Young Child: A How-to-do-it Manual.* New York: Neal Schuman Publishers, 1995.

Ernst, Linda L. *Lapsit Services for the Very Young II: A How-to-do-it Manual.* New York: Neal Schuman Publishers, 2001.

Feinberg, Sandra and Kathleen Deere. *Running a Parent-Child Workshop. A How-to-do-it Manual*. New York: Neal Schuman Publishers, 1995.

Folkmanis Puppets. Folkmanis, Inc. 1219 Park Avenue, Emeryville, Calif. 94608, (510) 658-7677, www.folkmanis.com. *Puppets can be ordered online, through a catalogue or through many retailers or suppliers.*

Greene, Ellin. *Books, Babies and Libraries. Serving Infants, Toddlers, their Parents and Caregivers*. Chicago: American Library Association, 1991.

Jeffrey, Debby Ann. *Literate Beginnings: Programs for Babies and Toddlers*. Chicago: American Library Association, 1995.

Marino, Jane & Dorothy F. Houlihan. *Mother Goose Time: Library Programs for Babies and Their Caregivers*. Photographs by Susan G. Drinker. Bronx, NY: H. W. Wilson, 1992.

Nespeca, Sue McCleaf. *Library Programming for Families with Young Children*. New York: Neal-Schuman, 1994.

Nichols, Judy. *Storytimes for Two-Year-Olds*. Illustrated by Lori D. Sears. 2d edition. Chicago: American Library Association, 1998.

Pat-a-Cake and Other Play Rhymes. Compiled by Joanna Cole and Stephanie Calmenson. Illustrated by Alan Tiegreen. New York: Morrow Junior Books, 1992.

Programming for Young Children: Birth through Age Five. Association for Library Service to Children. Prepared by Carole D. Fiore and Sue McCleaf Nespeca. Chicago: American Library Association, 1996.

Ra, Carol F. *Trot, Trot to Boston. Play Rhymes for Baby*. Pictures by Catherine Stock. New York: Lothrop, Lee & Shepard, 1987.

Ring a Ring O' Roses: Finger Plays for Pre-School Children. Compiled by the Flint Public Library. Tenth Edition. Flint, MI: Flint Public Library, 1996.

Stetson, Emily and Vicky Congdon. *Little Hands Fingerplays & Action Songs: Seasonal Activities & Creative Play for 2–6 Year Olds*. Illustrated by Betsy Day. Charlotte VT: Williamson Publishing, 2001.

What Works. Developmentally Appropriate Library Programming for Very Young Children. Edited by Jane Marino. Albany: New York Library Association, Youth Services Section, 1999.

Yolen, Jane, editor. *The Lap-Time Song and Play Book*. Musical arrangements by Adam Stemple. Pictures by Marget Tomes. San Diego: Harcourt, Brace, Jovanovich, 1989.

PROGRAMS AND INITIATIVES THAT SUPPORT EARLY CHILDHOOD LITERACY

The programs profiled here are only a few of the programs in existence. Their example may give you inspiration to apply for a grant or simply provide examples of how to reach out to your own community in order to promote reading in very young children and to continue to welcome babies into your library.

Beginning with Books Center for Early Literacy. Founded in 1964, Beginning with Books was developed to change the disparity in reading ability and enjoyment between those who had grown up with books and those who had not. It offers children books, information, and the encouragement they need to begin a habit of daily home reading to low-income parents. A nonprofit affiliate of the Carnegie Library of Pittsburgh, its programs operate in partnership with other organizations that serve low-income families. Beginning with Books, 5920 Kirkwood Street, Pittsburgh, PA 15206 *www.beginningwithbooks.org.*

Born to Read. Born to Read was begun in 1995 by ALSC, the Association for Library Service to Children, a division of the American Library Association, and initially funded by a grant from the Prudential Foundation. The program's goals were to develop models of library and health-care-provider partnerships and demonstrate how these two organizations can work together to further the goal of literacy. It seeks to help parents improve their reading skills and teach them the importance of reading to their children and to promote greater public awareness of health and parenting resources available in libraries. Brochures are available from ALSC. Born to Read Project/Association for Library Service to Children, 50 E. Huron St., Chicago, IL 60611. *www.ala.org/alsc/ born.html.*

Public Library Association's Early Literacy Initiative. Begun in 2000, with a partnership with the National Institute of Child Health and Human Development, the initiative seeks to develop model public library programs incorporating research-based findings on reading development in children. With these programs, the initiative hopes to enlist parents and caregivers as partners in preparing their children for learning to read and to provide the most effective methods to achieve that goal. In 2001, ALSC and PLA formed a partnership to pilot these materials in public libraries across the country. These pilot programs are still ongoing and reports will be sent to the public library community on them. Public Library Association, American Library Association, 50 E. Huron St., Chicago, IL 60611 1-800-545-2433 ext. 5PLA *www.pla.org/projects/preschool/preschool_overview.html.*

OTHER ORGANIZATIONS TO KNOW

National Association for the Education of Young Children. Founded in 1926, NAEYC has over 100,000 members and a national network of nearly 450 local, state, and regional affiliates. It is the largest organization of early childhood educators and other professionals dedicated to improving the quality of children's programs from birth through grade three. NAEYC, P.O. Box 97156, Washington D.C. 20090-7156 *www.naeyc.org.*

Zero to Three. The nation's leading resource on the first three years of life, this nonprofit organization's goal is to strengthen and support families, professionals, and communities to promote the healthy development of babies and toddlers. Zero to Three, National Center for Infants, Toddlers and Families, 2000 M. Street, NW, Suite 200, Washington, DC 200367. *www.zerotothree.org.*

INDEX

SELECTED REFERENCES

"Away up High in the Apple Tree" from *Wibbleton to Wobbleton* by Sally Jaeger. Copyright 1998, by 49 North Productions, Inc. 25 Eaton Ave. Toronto, Canada, M4J2Z4.

"Bye Low, My Baby" from *Wibbleton to Wobbleton* by Sally Jaeger. Copyright 1998, by 49 North Productions, Inc. 25 Eaton Ave. Toronto, Canada, M4J2Z4.

"Fee, Fie, Foe, Fum" from *Ring a Ring o' Roses* published by the Flint Public Library, 1026 E. Kearsley St., Flint, MI. 48502. www.flint.lib.mi.us.

"Go to Sleepy Baby Bye" from *Wibbleton to Wobbleton* by Sally Jaeger. Copyright 1998, by 49 North Productions, Inc. 25 Eaton Ave. Toronto, Canada, M4J2Z4.

"I Clap My Hands" from *Ring a Ring o' Roses* published by the Flint Public Library, 1026 E. Kearsley St., Flint, MI. 48502. www.flint.lib.mi.us.

"A Little Frog" from *Ring a Ring o' Roses* published by the Flint Public Library, 1026 E. Kearsley St., Flint, MI. 48502. www.flint.lib.mi.us.

"1,2,3,4,5, My Little Baby Pie" from *Wibbleton to Wobbleton* by Sally Jaeger. 49 North Productions 25 Eaton Ave. Toronto, Canada, M4J2Z4. Copyright 1997, by Sally Jaeger. Used by permission of Sally Jaeger.

"Rub-a-Dub Dub" from *Wibbleton to Wobbleton* by Sally Jaeger. 49 North Productions 25 Eaton Ave. Toronto, Canada, M4J2Z4. Copyright 1998, by Sally Jaeger. Used by permission of Sally Jaeger.

"Ten Little Gentlemen" from *Mr. Bear Says Hello* by Sally Jaeger. Copyright 2000 by 49 North Productions 25 Eaton Ave. Toronto, Canada, M4J2Z4.

"Rain is Falling Down" from *Mr. Bear Says Hello* by Sally Jaeger. Copyright 2000 by 49 North Productions. 25 Eaton Ave. Toronto, Canada, M4J2Z4.

"Roll, Roll, Roll Your Hands" from *Toddlers on Parade,* by Carol Hammett and Elaine Bueffel with musical arrangements by Dennis Buck. Copyright 1985 by Kimbo Educational, P.O. Box 477, 10 North Third Ave., Long Branch, NJ 07740. Used by permission of Kimbo Educational.

"Say, Say Oh Baby" from *Baby Games,* by Priscilla Hegner, with musical arrangements by Dennis Buck. Copyright 1997 by Kimbo Educational, P.O. Box 477, 10 North Third Ave., Long Branch, NJ 07740. Used by permission of Kimbo Educational.

"Wiggle Wiggle Fingers" from *Ring a Ring o' Roses* published by the Flint Public Library, 1026 E. Kearsley St., Flint, MI. 48502. www.flint.lib.mi.us.

ABOUT THE AUTHOR

Jane Marino is the Head of Children's Services at the Scarsdale Public Library in Scarsdale New York. She is the author of two other books on infant and toddler programming and has spoken to librarians in many states about the importance of infant and toddler programming.

An active member of ALSC, a division of the American Library Association, she has served on the 2000 Caldecott Committee and as chair of the Parent Education and Preschool Services Committee. She also served as guest editor for the Winter 2002 edition of ALSC's Journal of Youth Services which had as its theme, "Early Childhood and Family Literacy."

As an active member of the New York Library Association, she served as editor of *What Works: Developmentally Appropriate Library Programs for Very Young Children*, published by the New York Library Association in 1999. She also is a book reviewer for *School Library Journal*.

APR 2007